HEALTH REPORTS:
DISEASES AND DISORDERS

ANOREXIA
AND BULIMIA

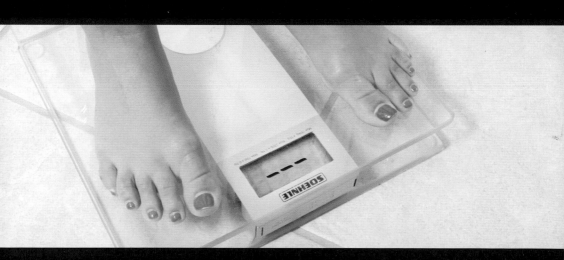

CAROL SONENKLAR

TWENTY-FIRST CENTURY BOOKS
MINNEAPOLIS

Twenty-First Century Books
A division of Lerner Publishing Group, Inc.
241 First Avenue North
Minneapolis, MN 55401 U.S.A.

Website address: www.lernerbooks.com

Library of Congress Cataloging-in-Publication Data

Sonenklar, Carol.
    Anorexia and bulimia / by Carol Sonenklar.
        p.   cm. — (USA Today health reports: Diseases and disorders)
    Includes bibliographical references and index.
    ISBN 978–0–8225–6786–8 (lib. bdg. : alk. paper)
    1. Anorexia nervosa—Popular works. 2. Bulimia—Popular works.
    I. Title.
    RC552.A5S66 2011
    616.85'26—dc22   2009052608

Manufactured in the United States of America
1 – DP – 7/15/10

CONTENTS

USA TODAY
HEALTH REPORTS:
DISEASES AND DISORDERS

MEET ANA AND MIA

EMMA'S STORY

Emma had made up the plan when she was a little girl. She was going to have a straight-A average, be the class valedictorian, and go to an Ivy League college. She managed to stay on that path. In her senior year in high school, she had a 4.0 average, was a National Merit Scholar, played field hockey, had a job, and was on the debating team. She sent applications to Harvard, Yale, Princeton, and Brown. Although these schools were highly competitive, Emma wasn't worried. She had everything under control.

Then things began to change at home. Emma's father started to travel frequently for work, and her mother was not happy about it. She heard them fighting late at night. Her mother's hours were cut back because business was so slow. Emma noticed that her mother started drinking more wine than usual. When Emma asked about it, her mother got angry and told her it was none of her business. Emma worried that her parents might divorce.

One night, Emma's parents were fighting as she tried to study for her calculus midterm exam. It was hard to concentrate. The next morning, for the first time ever, Emma felt she was not prepared for a test. But she reminded herself that she was a star math student. There was no need to worry.

The test was harder than Emma had expected. If she got a B, her final grade probably wouldn't suffer. She would just have to do some extra credit and ace the final. No problem.

When the calculus teacher handed back the tests, Emma was stunned. She had gotten a D. She felt her stomach turn over when she saw the grade. She couldn't believe it. Emma was close to tears but managed to control herself until the end of class. Then she ran to the girl's bathroom, locked herself in a stall, and sobbed. Emma felt as though her life was spiraling out of control. She didn't know what to do.

SAM'S STORY

When Sam discovered wrestling, a whole new world opened up to him. He'd always been small and was never picked for teams. He was well coordinated and strong, but he would often choke when it was his turn at bat or when he tried to shoot a basket.

Sam was in his freshman year of college and was one of two wrestlers in the 150-pound (68-kilogram) class. The other, Cody Goodman, was a junior. Sam knew that Cody used to be in the 175-pound (79 kg) class, but he'd lost weight and was in really good shape. Cody was one of the team's stars. Sam didn't get to wrestle as much as he would have liked. He wished the coach would choose him more often. But he was okay with being number two. He had time.

Sam's first wrestling match was better than he'd expected. He and his opponent tied and went into an overtime round. Sam eventually held his opponent in a fall for two seconds. All his hard work and practice had paid off. The crowd in the gym was standing and cheering. His parents had driven up for the match, and they were thrilled. Sam loved being part of a team. He started eating lunch with some of the other wrestlers and was soon socializing almost exclusively with them.

Sam's coach always lectured the team on the importance of maintaining their weight. Everyone was weighed every day at practice. If someone had put on 1 or 2 pounds (0.5 or 0.9 kg), the coach was not happy. One day, when a wrestler in the 115-pound (52 kg) class weighed in and had gained weight, the coach gave the team an earful. He said that there was no chance they would make the state finals

if they weren't tough enough to maintain their weight. "Wrestling is about emotional and physical toughness," the coach said. "If you can't hack it, this is not the sport for you."

Sam listened intently. He had never thought about his weight before joining the team. He just ate what he wanted. Some of the guys told him how lucky he was to not have to worry about it. "So listen up, all of you," the coach continued. "You mess up on two weigh-ins, you're not going to be playing much. Do what you need to do to win." They all got the message.

EVA'S STORY

Eva's family moved from Phoenix, Arizona, to Denver, Colorado, when she was in eighth grade. Her mother told her there would be plenty of Latina girls at her new school. And she was right. There were quite a few Latino students. They all hung out together. They did not mix with the other kids. Eva sometimes ate lunch with them. It bothered her that just because she was Latina, she wasn't "allowed" to be friends with other people.

Eva's weight had been pretty normal until she hit thirteen. That's when it became harder to fit into her size 2 jeans. She tried to explain to her mother that she didn't want to

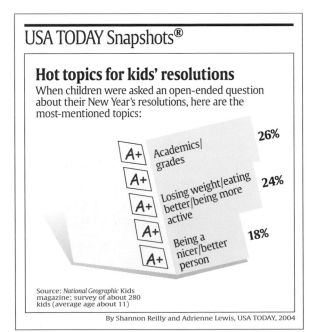

USA TODAY Snapshots®

Hot topics for kids' resolutions
When children were asked an open-ended question about their New Year's resolutions, here are the most-mentioned topics:

A+ Academics/grades — 26%

A+ Losing weight/eating better/being more active — 24%

A+ Being a nicer/better person — 18%

Source: *National Geographic* Kids magazine; survey of about 280 kids (average age about 11)

By Shannon Reilly and Adrienne Lewis, USA TODAY, 2004

eat what the family always ate: cheese empanadas and tamales, spicy chorizos, and burritos. It wasn't that she didn't like the food. She loved it. But it was high in calories and Eva did not want to gain weight. The most popular girls in the school were blonde with perfect, tiny bodies. They wore size 0. That's what Eva wanted to be. She wanted to look like a model.

Eva became depressed and spent more and more time alone in her room. She hated how she looked. When her mother asked her what was wrong, she wouldn't tell her. She would study herself in the mirror for hours. She hated her black hair, olive skin, and nose. She knew her mother would be ashamed of her for feeling this way. She always talked about how proud Eva should be of her family and heritage.

WHAT ARE ANOREXIA AND BULIMIA

Ana always tells me I'm fat. She's right. And thank goodness Mia's there to help when I eat something and regret it. Ana and Mia are the only ones I can trust.

Ana and Mia are pretty nasty girls. Ana is highly critical, and Mia only wants to be a friend at certain times. But Ana and Mia are not real girls. These names are short for the two eating disorders that are the focus of this book: *anorexia nervosa* (Ana) and *bulimia* (Mia). Anorexia nervosa, commonly called anorexia, is an eating disorder in which people intentionally starve themselves. People with bulimia binge and purge. This means they eat a large quantity of food in a short time and then try to get rid of the food by forcing themselves to vomit. Other methods of purging include taking laxatives, which stimulate the bowels, and overexercising. Anorexia and bulimia are serious disorders that need medical and psychological treatment.

For many people suffering from these disorders, Ana and Mia are real. These people believe that Ana and Mia speak to them. They criticize and scold. Ana and Mia tell them what to eat and what not to eat.

People with eating disorders have strong feelings and attitudes about eating. They do things to their bodies that can have life-threatening consequences. People with anorexia or bulimia are constantly worried about their weight and how they look.

Humans have a complex relationship with food. It is about much more than basic survival. We associate happy times with food. We look forward to birthday parties with cake and ice cream; Thanksgiving dinners of turkey, stuffing, and pumpkin pie; and grilling burgers and hot dogs in the summertime. People often use food as a reward or to provide comfort, especially in times of stress.

This family is sharing a Thanksgiving feast. Food is often a large part of celebrations and holidays.

At family dinners, we come together to share daily experiences. The feeling of fullness and being satisfied brings a sense of calm. Food is also often the focus of social gatherings. Going out for a snack after school or meeting a friend for coffee is much more than eating or drinking. These activities strengthen bonds and help us to connect with others.

Our ancestors knew what it was to be hungry for days or weeks. To keep from being hungry, they sought new places to live, risked their lives hunting animals, or even went to war. But in modern times, most people in Western nations (the wealthy countries of Europe and North America) never have to be hungry for very long. We live in an era of plenty. Food is generally easy to find.

People are born with a basic instinct to seek food when they are hungry. It's simple: I am hungry, so I eat. But it is not that simple for some people. When they think about food or eating, they are fraught with anxiety, fear, or panic. These people don't want to eat and think of reasons to avoid it. Or they might eat too much and then feel they have to punish themselves afterward.

For these individuals, food is an enemy. Instead of eating when they are hungry and stopping when they're full, they have strong responses to food. They are frightened and cannot stop thinking about it. They keep food in their pockets or hide it in their bedrooms. They wait until everyone is asleep at night and stuff themselves with whatever is in the refrigerator. They have lost the ability to perceive eating for what it is—a means of staying healthy and alive.

A person with an eating disorder develops a distorted body image. Body image is an individual's perception of how he or she looks. The disorder prevents people from having a realistic sense of how they look and what they should eat. When they look into a mirror, they do not see their true reflection. They see inadequacy, weakness, and failure.

www.usatoday.com

USA TODAY

Life
SECTION D

October 13, 2009

From the Pages of USA TODAY

Tweens ponder body image
Summit brings girls together for support, learning

When 12-year-old Chloe Harris sees a large-screen image of a stick-thin model in a new ad campaign, the seventh-grader from Alexandria, Va., says the picture makes her "feel sick" because the model looks so "unnormal."

Her reaction is on target, says body-image expert Jess Weiner, who speaks about the eating disorders that began for her at age 11.

"Every single person here wonders whether they've got the right body or the right look," says Weiner, who writes a body-image column for *Seventeen* magazine. She spoke to more than 200 tween girls, ages 9-14, gathered for the first National Tween Girl Summit here over the weekend.

Ultra-thin models and celebrities are getting some backlash these days, but body image is still a major preoccupation for girls. Some marketers have started to respond, such as Dove, a summit sponsor, which created the Campaign for Real Beauty and the Dove Self-Esteem Fund.

Researchers are particularly interested in the link between self-esteem, body image and eating disorders, and new studies are trying to better explain the connection.

What others think

A study was published this summer in the journal *Child Development* by researchers at the University of Oregon and University of California-Los Angeles who conducted brain scans on 12 young people ages 11 to 13 and on an equal number of young adults ages 22 to 30. During the imaging, the participants responded to 40 questions about their popularity and their academics. They were asked about whether phrases such as "I am popular" described them, and whether others would agree. Compared with the young adults, the study suggests that a tween's self-image is largely based on how she believes others see her.

"If you ask them what they think of themselves, they can't separate that from what other people think of them," says Jennifer Pfeifer, an assistant professor of psychology in Oregon. "Whenever you ask them about themselves, they immediately engage in thinking about what others think of them."

In a study about weight and body satisfaction, researchers measured the height and weight of 4,254 schoolchildren from Nova Scotia [Canada] and asked them how much they agreed with the statement "I like the way I look."

"We found in children as young as 10 and 11—all fifth-graders—they're experiencing these very negative feelings about their bodies related to their weight," says researcher S. Bryn Austin, assistant professor in pediatrics at Children's Hospital in Boston. "It was true in both boys and girls, but it was more pronounced in girls. In the boys, being very thin was also related to feeling bad about their body, but the thinner for girls, the better they felt about their bodies."

The study, done with researchers from Harvard University and the University of Alberta in Canada, was published in August in the journal *BMC Public Health*.

Parents' words matter

Psychology professor Joan Chrisler of Connecticut College in New London, Conn., says teasing or even well-meaning remarks by a parent can damage a child's self-image.

"The things we say about ourselves in front of our daughters and the way we treat our own bodies really has an effect on our girls," says Dara Chadwick of Jamestown, R.I., author of *You'd Be So Pretty If . . . : Teaching Our Daughters to Love Their Bodies—Even When We Don't Love Our Own.*

Heather Moran of Mantua, N.J., brought her daughter Erin, 13, to the summit, along with one of Erin's friends. Moran says she has lost 35 pounds [16 kg] and ran a half-marathon in Philadelphia [Pennsylvania] last month.

"I was turning 40 and I wanted to feel good," Moran says. "I don't think she saw it as body image. She saw it as me just wanting to be healthy."

Sophia Cucci, 11, of Harrington Park, N.J., came to the summit with her mother, Michele.

What Sophia learned from the presentations: "Not to base your life on people in magazines or TV shows, because that's not really how they look."

Psychotherapist Jill Rutledge of Evanston, Ill., author of the 2007 book *Picture Perfect: What You Need to Feel Better About Your Body*, urges mothers to "hold their tongues when their daughter is eating something they wouldn't eat. Eating a brownie isn't a horrible thing."

—Sharon Jayson

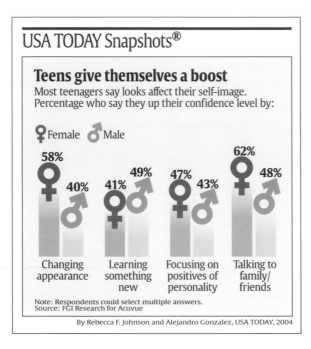

USA TODAY Snapshots®

Teens give themselves a boost
Most teenagers say looks affect their self-image.
Percentage who say they up their confidence level by:

♀ Female   ♂ Male

58%
40%

41%
49%

47%
43%

62%
48%

Changing appearance

Learning something new

Focusing on positives of personality

Talking to family/ friends

Note: Respondents could select multiple answers.
Source: FGI Research for Acuvue

By Rebecca F. Johnson and Alejandro Gonzalez, USA TODAY, 2004

The causes of these disorders are complex. Something usually triggers an eating disorder. It might be a family crisis, an emotional rejection, abuse, or some other psychological disorder. To feel as if they are in control of their lives, people with eating disorders react to these triggers by controlling what they eat.

In the United States, about ten million females and one million males suffer from eating disorders. (Eating disorders other than anorexia and bulimia make up a small percentage of the total.) Doctors know that millions suffer in silence. Many people are embarrassed to admit they have an eating disorder.

People of all ages and cultures suffer from anorexia and bulimia. There are reports of cases in individuals from as young as five and as old as seventy. In most cases, the disorder begins in adolescence and affects the emotional and physical well-being of the sufferer over time.

Anorexia and bulimia require serious treatment by a team of professionals. But sometimes, even that is not enough. Even with treatment, the conditions often do not completely disappear. Many adolescents and young women and men struggle throughout their lives to maintain healthy eating habits and attitudes. But people can overcome these disorders if they receive treatment.

Eating disorders are on the rise in every age group. Watching a loved one suffer from anorexia or bulimia is frightening and bewildering. This book will help you understand what causes eating disorders and why they are so difficult to conquer.

CHAPTER ONE

EATING BEHAVIORS THROUGH HISTORY

Voluntary starvation has always attracted attention. In ancient Japan, a man could humiliate his enemy by "fasting against him," literally starving on his doorstep. During the twelfth and thirteenth centuries A.D., self-starvation was considered a religious act, particularly among Western Christians. These so-called holy anorexics were women who starved themselves to "cleanse their spirits" and become closer to God. One of these women, Saint Catherine of Siena, believed that yielding to hunger was yielding to sin.

In sixteenth-century England, "miraculous maids" claimed to be able to live without nourishment. These women usually came from poor families in rural areas. As news of their miraculous existence spread, people paid to see them. Some of these young women were found to be frauds. Others died of malnutrition.

English physician Richard Morton described a condition caused by "sadness and anxious cares" in 1689. Reporting two cases, he wrote that one was a "sad and anxious girl who pored over books." The second was a boy who was "prone to studying too hard." The girl and boy Morton described both strove for perfection. This is one of the main characteristics of anorexics.

People have used hunger strikes to bring attention to particular causes. Mohandas Gandhi, a political and spiritual leader of India in the early twentieth century, fasted as part of his campaign for India's independence from Great Britain. Bobby Sands of Northern Ireland led a hunger strike while imprisoned in 1981 to protest conditions for political prisoners. He died on the sixty-sixth day of the strike. In 2010 Cuban dissident Guillermo Fariñas refused food and water to protest the death of jailed hunger striker Orlando Zapata and demand the release of all political prisoners in Cuba. Fariñas had served eleven years in prison and staged more than twenty hunger strikes between 1995 and 2009.

A HISTORY OF ANOREXIA

In 1865 an English dictionary defined anorexia as "an absence of appetite." It specified that this condition was not accompanied by dislike of food. Most nineteenth-century doctors assumed that a lack of appetite in a sick person was just a symptom of another illness. It was not recognized as a disorder until it was seen in wealthier families that had access to health care.

Mohandas Gandhi used hunger strikes for political purposes in the early twentieth century.

British physician Dr. William Gull published the first medical report on the disorder in 1868, in a paper titled "Anorexia Nervosa." At the time, Gull was an important and powerful doctor within the social circle of England's queen, Victoria. He identified the common medical symptom of a lack of appetite as a disorder. Gull's description of anorexia also targeted a specific group: females between the ages of sixteen and twenty-three.

Charles Lasègue, a French neurologist, identified and described what he called *l'anorexie hystérique* (hysterical anorexia) in an April 1873 publication. At the time, the word *hysterical* described emotional problems that affected only women. Lasègue focused

on the mental stages the patient passed through. Gull focused on "simple starvation" and rejected Lasègue's use of the term *hysterical*. Gull preferred *anorexia nervosa*, which referred to a disorder of the central nervous system. Gull's diagnosis of anorexia nervosa was based on whether the menstrual cycle stopped (which almost always happens with female anorexics) or did not appear in the first place. The anorexic's lack of appetite, Gull thought, was caused by a diseased mental state and not by a digestive disorder. To treat anorexia, Gull suggested removing the patient from the parents' home. He had observed that anxious parents gave in when the anorexic did not want to eat. They would excuse their child from eating rather than experiencing the sometimes violent episodes that would occur if they forced the issue.

ADOLESCENT GIRLS AND HYSTERIA

In the 1800s, children in poor families often had to leave their homes to work. But middle-class sons and daughters in the United States, Britain, and France lived with their parents until they married and moved to a home of their own. Many parents viewed their daughters as the jewels of their families. Parents thought daughters were delicate and fragile beings who needed protection and guidance.

At the time, parents made decisions for their daughters about clothing, friends, activities, and mates. The intense pressure to marry sometimes led to anger and unhappiness in the young women. They felt they had no say in their futures. This feeling of a lack of control is often found in people who develop eating disorders. In his paper on hysteria, Charles Lasègue told of an adolescent girl who manipulated her family by refusing to eat. He believed this behavior symbolized a conflict between maturing daughters and their families. By refusing food, young women could make a bold statement without seeming unfeminine.

HILDE BRUCH: EATING DISORDER PIONEER

In 1933 Hilde Bruch, a young German doctor, immigrated to the United Kingdom because of rising anti-Semitism (discrimination against Jews) in her native country. Bruch was a practicing pediatrician. She began to research childhood obesity in 1937. She then left pediatrics to study psychiatry at Johns Hopkins University in Baltimore, Maryland. She eventually opened a private psychiatric practice and joined the faculty of Columbia University in New York City. In the 1960s, Bruch became interested in anorexia nervosa and began to develop her own theories about the disorder.

Bruch observed that her anorexic patients were lacking a sense of self. Bruch discovered through interviews that her patients felt helpless in every part of their lives. Controlling their bodies was a desperate attempt to eliminate the feeling of complete powerlessness.

In 1978 Bruch published *The Golden Cage: The Enigma of Anorexia Nervosa.* In the book, the golden cage represented the middle-class homes of her young patients. She believed they felt trapped. Bruch also found that all her patients with anorexia had distorted perceptions of their appearance. They also did not recognize how much damage they were doing to their bodies by refusing to eat. Bruch developed a new type of therapy that focused on listening to patients. This so-called active listening approach helped patients with self-esteem issues. Lack of self-esteem is basic to anorexia.

At that time, it was assumed that eating disorders affected only affluent young women. But this wasn't entirely true. Doctors didn't know much about the disorder in the 1970s. Only a few doctors treated it, and their patients were all from upper-class, white families. So people assumed that girls from these kinds of families were the only ones to suffer from eating disorders.

With the publication of Bruch's book in 1978, cases of reported anorexia increased. In 1983 one of the country's most famous singers, Karen Carpenter, died of anorexia. Then the public began to truly understand the seriousness of eating disorders. Even so, it

Karen Carpenter

Brother and sister Richard and Karen Carpenter were a singing duo. The Carpenters were one of the most popular musical acts of the late 1970s and early 1980s.

Karen *(opposite page)* had always been a talented musician. She played the accordion, the flute, and the drums. The siblings struggled before becoming famous—forming bands and then breaking up. At first, Karen played the drums but did not sing. With her brother's encouragement, she started singing—and the duo took off. When music executives at A&M Records heard her, they immediately offered the Carpenters a contract.

Karen had been a chubby teenager. As she got older, she was determined to lose weight. The dieting began in 1967, when Karen was seventeen. She went from 140 to 120 pounds (64 to 54 kg). She continued to lose weight. By 1975 Karen was down to 80 pounds (36 kg). This was happening at the same time that the Carpenter's single "Close to You" was a gigantic hit. It reached number one in the United States in only six weeks. Her took many more years for women and girls from different ethnic and economic backgrounds to admit their condition and seek help.

More recently, in an effort to help others, several celebrities have spoken out about their battles with anorexia. Actresses Jane Fonda, Lynn Redgrave, Christina Ricci, Kate Winslet, and Mary-Kate Olsen are among those who have shared their experiences and sought help.

brother, Richard, said, "Although her voice was never affected, you could hear gasps from the audience when she came onstage, and there was considerable mail from fans asking what was wrong."

In 1975, while performing in Las Vegas, Nevada, Karen collapsed in the middle of a song and was rushed to the hospital. She began treatment for anorexia in 1982 and managed to get her weight up to 110 pounds (50 kg). She and her family were certain she was recovering. But the years of starvation, medication, and laxatives had taken a toll. Her brother believed she had gained her weight back too fast, which put a strain on her heart. Karen was in the midst of recording the duo's twelfth album with him when she died of a heart attack at her parent's home. Karen Carpenter was thirty-two years old.

How Common Are Eating Disorders?

According to the National Eating Disorders Association:

Five to ten million girls and women in the United States and one million boys and men suffer from eating disorders.

• Forty percent of newly identified cases of anorexia are in girls between the ages of fifteen and nineteen.

• The number of reported cases of anorexia in young women aged fifteen to nineteen years has risen in each decade since 1930.

• The number of reported cases of bulimia in females aged ten to thirty-nine tripled between 1988 and 1993.

• Only one-third of people with anorexia receive mental health care. Only 6 percent of people with bulimia receive mental health care.

• The majority of people with eating disorders do not receive adequate care.

• Four out of ten Americans know someone who has suffered from an eating disorder.

A HISTORY OF BULIMIA

Accounts tell of Romans in the second and fourth centuries A.D. who tickled their throats so they could vomit and continue feasting. In 1797 *Encyclopaedia Britannica* defined *bulimia* as "an intense preoccupation with food, combined with overeating at short intervals, followed by bouts of vomiting." Like anorexia, bulimia was long considered a symptom of another disease. Gull and Lasègue both noted that some of their anorexic patients would force themselves to vomit. Medical reports told of women who ate in secret and stole food to eat later.

In the early twentieth century, accounts told of people who ate a large amount quickly, or binged, and then vomited, or purged. After World War II (1939–1945), a shift in the Western definition of female beauty occurred. To be beautiful, a woman had to be

Left: Betty Grable defined the ideal American beauty in the 1930s and early 1940s. *Right:* In the early 2000s, the ideal has shifted to a much taller and much thinner woman, such as this model on a catwalk in 2010.

October 6, 1997

From the Pages of USA TODAY

Teen Girls No Longer Enjoy an Age of Innocence

Excerpt from the diary of a young teenage girl in 1892:

Resolved, not to talk about myself or feelings. To think before speaking. To work seriously. To be self restrained in conversation and actions. Not to let my thoughts wander. To be dignified. Interest myself more in others.

Excerpt from the diary of a young teenage girl in 1982:

I will try to make myself better in any way I possibly can with the help of my budget and babysitting money. I will lose weight, get new lenses, already got new haircut, good makeup, new clothes and accessories.

In the late 1960s, a 16-year-old wrote in her diary: "I'm too ugly. I'm too fat. I have a crummy personality." She was 5-foot-4 [162 centimeters] and weighed 120 pounds [54 kg], had friends, lots of dates and good grades. Yet her self-esteem depended on her weight and her goal was to be 10 pounds [4.5 kg] lighter so she could look "halfway decent."

—*Anita Manning*

thin. The general public felt that extra weight was disgraceful and indicated a lack of self-control. Doctors reported that some patients said they were ashamed of being fat. These people often engaged in self-starvation or bingeing and purging.

In the 1970s, doctors became more aware of patients who gorged themselves on food but remained at a normal weight. The first description of this behavior as separate from anorexia was by Dr. Gerald Russell, a British physician. Russell called bulimia "an ominous variant" of anorexia. He listed three signs that doctors should look for:

episodic overeating, laxative overuse, and fear of fatness. Russell also believed that female students attending universities were the most likely to be bulimic. Bulimia was thought to be a concern only of wealthy families in Western countries.

USA TODAY Snapshots®

What's up doc?
Top five issues that parents consider very important for health care providers to discuss with adolescents:

Diet/nutrition — 77%
Exercise/sports — 67%
Physical changes of puberty — 61%
Drug use — 57%
Tobacco use — 54%

Source: Knowledge Networks survey of 2,060 adults for the C.S. Mott Children's Hospital National Poll on Children's Health.

By Michelle Healy and Dave Merrill, USA TODAY, 2008

CHAPTER TWO

DEFINING ANOREXIA AND BULIMIA

Emma was lying in bed one morning. She was awake, thinking about the chemistry test she had at the end of the week. She was worried. What if she didn't do well? Then she heard a voice.

"Of course, you won't do well."

It was a voice in her head but different from her usual thoughts.

"You're stupid. You'll probably fail the test."

The voice was sharp and mocking.

"I know the truth about you, Emma. You've fooled everyone else for a long, long, time, haven't you?"

Emma got out of bed. She needed to get ready for school. She went to the bathroom, washed her face, and brushed her teeth. She could hear her mother downstairs. Her father had moved out about a month earlier. She missed him, even though they still had dinner twice a week. She didn't know what to talk about with her father. He didn't seem interested in her life anymore. Neither did her mother. She was either working at the bookstore or looking for work. She was hardly ever home. When she was home, she complained about Emma's father, how much her feet hurt, and how awful her boss was. Emma tried to avoid her as much as she could.

Emma slipped on her blue jeans and a sweater. She brushed her hair and put on some lip gloss.

"Let's face it: you're not just stupid, you're ugly too."

Emma knew the voice was right.

"You're ugly because you're fat."

Emma had always been athletic. She had never been skinny, but she had never been fat. Some of her friends were always dieting, but not her. Her father always told her she looked great—not like those girls who were too skinny and always talking about themselves. But it had *been a long time since her father had said anything like that. Emma thought it was because she didn't look great anymore.*

The voice continued, "You're so ugly and fat you should just go away. You're a failure at everything. No one can stand looking at you." Emma knew this was true. She picked up her backpack and walked downstairs. When her mother told her breakfast was ready, Emma said she wasn't hungry. She left the house.

"That's right. You're fat. You don't need any food."

WHAT IS ANOREXIA?

The word *anorexia* comes from the Greek words *an*, which means "not," and *orexis*, "appetite" or "desire." *Nervosa* means "having to do with the nerves." People with anorexia exhibit extreme behaviors toward food and eating. Anorexics are deathly afraid of gaining weight. Anorexics starve themselves. Although it is an obsession with the physical body, anorexia does not have a physical cause. It is a complicated emotional, psychological, and biological disorder that affects the body.

Anorexia is often a physical reaction to things such as stress, anxiety, unhappiness, and perceived lack of control. People with anorexia are often intensely hungry. But they deny hunger, make excuses to avoid eating, or hide food they claim to have eaten. Anorexics learn to control their appetites. They control their lives by not giving in to their hunger.

Women suffer from anorexia ten times more then men. People who participate in sports that require a slim figure, such as ballet, wrestling, gymnastics, or bodybuilding, are more likely to become anorexic than other people. Many anorexics are perfectionists and have a poor self-image. They may have been teased by others about general appearance or weight in particular. Some were sexually abused

as children. Others may have had digestive problems when they were young or come from a family with a history of eating disorders.

Anorexia can be a deadly disease. According to a study in the *Archives of General Psychiatry*, for U.S. females between the ages of fifteen and twenty-four, the number of deaths caused by anorexia is twelve times higher than the number of combined deaths from other causes.

HOW ANOREXIA BEGINS

Anorexia is sometimes triggered by a traumatic event. The breakup of a family, the loss of a parent, or a painful emotional rejection can lead to the beginnings of an eating disorder. Adolescence is an intensely emotional time, so anorexia can start from situations such as doing poorly in school, not being accepted into a group, or failing to make a team or club. Anorexics often feel bad about themselves in the first place. So when things go wrong, they assume it's their fault. Almost all anorexics suffer from low self-esteem.

Adolescence is a time when your body is changing. For girls this means fuller hips and breasts. Someone who feels that everything is bad in her life may use these physical changes as an excuse to go on a diet. Almost all cases of anorexia begin with a diet. Most adolescents eventually give up after a short time. They find that diets are difficult to stick to, especially when they're out with friends.

But some young women have a completely different experience with dieting. They succeed at losing weight and everyone notices. Because thinness is so prized in U.S. culture, other people, friends in particular, will notice and compliment a girl who loses weight. This makes her feel great about herself. She feels she is finally good at something—losing weight. Perhaps she becomes more popular and her friends are envious. More boys may notice her. She begins to focus on what she eats, forbidding certain foods that are high in fat or calories.

From the anorexic's point of view, she is now in control. Naturally, she wants all the praise and positive feedback to continue. So she stays on the diet and loses more weight. At some point, however, the young woman might lose perspective. Her weight loss begins to affect her mind and damage her body. To stay in control of her life, she continues the pattern and slowly starves herself.

TYPES OF ANOREXIA

There are three different kinds of anorexia. Some anorexics restrict food altogether, starving themselves (restriction starvation). Others binge and purge. And some control their weight with compulsive exercise. They cannot control the urge to exercise. Some anorexics might only have one of the three types. But often the three types of anorexia overlap.

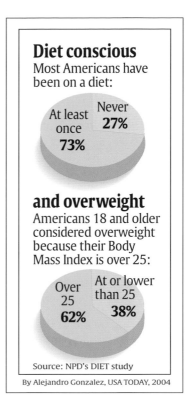

Diet conscious
Most Americans have been on a diet:

At least once **73%** Never **27%**

and overweight
Americans 18 and older considered overweight because their Body Mass Index is over 25:

Over 25 **62%** At or lower than 25 **38%**

Source: NPD's DIET study

By Alejandro Gonzalez, USA TODAY, 2004

Most people are familiar with the restriction-starvation type of anorexia. People with this type starve themselves. They allow themselves very few calories each day. They might use diet pills to control appetite or make excuses to avoid eating. In the purging type of anorexia, the sufferer purges food through vomiting, fasting, or abusing laxatives or enemas (an enema is a liquid introduced through the anus to stimulate evacuation of the bowels). This type of anorexia is similar to bulimia nervosa. Anorexics who exercise compulsively go beyond a healthy amount of exercise. They might do two hundred push-ups or five hundred sit-ups in a row. People with this type of anorexia will exercise no matter where they are or what the weather is. Often they must hide in a bedroom or bathroom to carry out their excessive exercise.

CHARACTERISTICS OF ANOREXIA

People with anorexia are obsessed with their weight and being thin. No one wants to be overweight, and many people watch what they eat. But anorexics take it further than that. Their notion of a desirable body

Staring at themselves in mirrors is a common behavior for anorexics—but they don't see themselves as they really are.

is far beyond a normal slender body. Many anorexics believe that if they become thin, they will be loved more. This desire to be thin and therefore loved is what drives many anorexics to excess. Anorexics must starve themselves to achieve a perfect degree of thinness. And it doesn't stop there. Once they've reached a weight goal, they continue to diet.

Many people with anorexia, such as Emma, hear voices inside their heads. Some call this voice Ana. The voice tells them that what they see in a mirror is false. No matter how skinny they are, how gaunt and wasted they have become, they are still fat. The voice tells them to spend a lot of time in front of mirrors examining every inch of their bodies. It is highly critical and prevents them from living in reality.

The voice tells anorexics that they are to blame for everything. It says that they are failures and that they deserve punishment. It criticizes them for being fat, worthless, and disgusting. It convinces them that giving in to their hunger is weak and that if they eat, they will not have control over their bodies and their lives. The voice tells them that being thin means happiness. If they tell anyone about

Diagnosing Anorexia

Anorexia is difficult to diagnose. Many people show only some of the signs of anorexia. Others have symptoms that are not necessarily related to anorexia. Doctors have come up with a list of things to identify anorexia. Someone with the following symptoms may be in the beginning stages of anorexia:

- A weight that is 15 percent lower than normal for height and age

- An intense fear of becoming fat

- A belief that the body is fat when it is very thin (a distorted body image)

- No period for three consecutive months

- Symptoms of one type of anorexia: binge/purge type, restriction-starvation type, or compulsive exercise type their problem, they will be punished by being force-fed.

Obsession with attaining perfection, combined with a distorted body image, makes it impossible for an anorexic to stop the cycle of dieting and weight loss. The voice, which is an anorexic's drive to starve herself, takes control.

Anorexics withdraw and live in a secret world of fear. They are afraid of getting fat, eating, and losing control. Anorexics forbid themselves to open up to others. Anorexics lie about their food intake. They tell worried parents that they ate a big lunch or ate at a friend's house to avoid meals at home. They also learn how to make food seem to disappear. They drop it under the table for a pet or wrap it in a napkin. They might cut everything into tiny pieces and move it around on the plate. Someone with anorexia will often exercise secretly, perhaps late at night. Anorexics will also hide what is happening to their bodies by wearing baggy clothes.

WHAT IS BULIMIA NERVOSA?

The word *bulimia* comes from the Greek word *bous*, which means "ox," and the Greek word *limos*, which means "hunger." So the word *bulimia* refers to someone who has an appetite as big as an ox or can eat an ox. Bulimia is an eating disorder in which the sufferer binges and then purges. Purging can mean vomiting, taking laxatives or diuretics (chemicals that increase the flow of urine), fasting, or exercising compulsively. People with bulimia sometimes feel guilty about their behavior and are depressed.

Worldwide, there are more cases of bulimia than anorexia. It is also more common in men than anorexia is. The things that trigger bulimia are similar to the things that trigger anorexia. These include dieting, puberty, life changes, and involvement in activities and work that require a slim physique.

Bulimia can be difficult to diagnose. Many bulimics are not overweight or underweight. They also go to great lengths to hide their eating and purging from others.

Eva could see that her parents were pleased she'd eaten a big dinner. They didn't know that right before dinner, she'd eaten two bags of cookies that she'd had under her bed. At dinner she had two empanadas, two helpings of beans and rice, and three pieces of corn bread. When dinner was over, Eva said that she had a big test the next day. Could she switch her night to do the dishes with her brother? Her mother said yes.

Eva went upstairs to her room. She shut the door loudly. A few seconds later, she opened the door quietly. Her family was still sitting around the table, talking. She went into the bathroom and turned on the water. Then she kneeled at the toilet and stuck her finger down her throat. She gagged several times, and then it worked. Eva vomited up her dinner and the cookies. After she was done, she brushed her teeth and fixed her hair. She felt great. She felt as if she'd gotten away with something really bad. She'd found a way to eat all she wanted without gaining weight.

THE CYCLE OF BINGEING AND PURGING

To binge means to eat an abnormally large amount of food in a very short time, usually within ten to fifteen minutes. Individuals feel out of control while eating. They feel as if they cannot stop or control themselves. But what is a large amount of food? A hamburger, french fries, and a soda total about 1,000 calories. That's a lot of food for some people, but not so much for others. For a petite female, it is close to an entire day's worth of calories. For a football player, swimmer, or someone with a very high metabolic rate, it's simply a meal.

Princess Diana, Bulimic

Diana, Princess of Wales *(opposite page)*, was the first wife of Charles, Prince of Wales, the heir to the British throne, and the mother of Princes William and Harry. Princess Diana suffered from bulimia for many years. She talked about it openly. Her bravery in coming forward helped many people confront their struggles with depression and eating disorders. The following is from a 1995 interview with Princess Diana that was shown on the public television show *Frontline*:

> The marriage [to Prince Charles] was the fairy tale of the century and the pressure to make it work was enormous. I was told that the media attention would fade, but it didn't. They began to focus very much on me; I seemed to be on the front of a newspaper every single day. It was ironic because the more the media focused on me, the more isolated I felt.
>
> I had so much pain inside me that I hurt myself on the outside. I wanted help, but people saw it as crying wolf or attention seeking. I hated the attention. I was actually crying out because I wanted to get better in order to go forward and continue my duty and my role as a wife and mother.
>
> I had bulimia for many years, and that is a secret type of illness. I felt badly about myself, as if I had no value as a person.

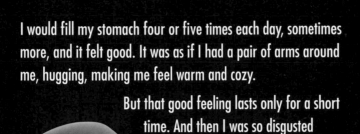

I would fill my stomach four or five times each day, sometimes more, and it felt good. It was as if I had a pair of arms around me, hugging, making me feel warm and cozy.

But that good feeling lasts only for a short time. And then I was so disgusted by my bulging stomach I made myself vomit. This repeats again and again. It was completely normal for me to come home and go straight to the fridge and start the eating and vomiting.

It was a symptom for what was going on in my marriage. I cried, I screamed for help, but with the wrong signals. People described my bulimia as a breach of etiquette: Diana is psychologically weak and unstable. But my husband and I didn't want to disappoint the public and it was better to do this than admit how unhappy I was.

A normal, healthy amount of food for an average adolescent or adult provides about 1,800 to 2,600 calories each day. During a binge episode, it would not be unusual for someone to eat twenty to twenty-five times that amount. That's more than 50,000 calories. It's equal to an entire extra-large pepperoni pizza, a tub of ice cream or a package of cookies, a bag of potato chips, and an entire cake. Bulimics might engage in this type of eating several times a day.

Bulimics binge just about anywhere—at work, at school, at home, and in restaurants. They will eat everything in the cupboards or the refrigerator. They might sneak food out of the house in the middle of the night to avoid getting caught. They will order large quantities of takeout food and pretend that more people are waiting to eat. Bulimics might drive to fast-food restaurants or convenience stores in different nearby towns so the employees do not recognize them. Bulimics who work in restaurants might take food from people's plates or hide some to take home. Bulimics might even go through dumpsters searching for food. Bulimics know that they are eating excessively and try to hide the behavior. Many binges occur at night, when everyone else is sleeping.

Bulimics almost always binge on junk food or fast food—ice cream, candy, cookies, chips, pizza, burgers, and french fries. Usually bulimics are on (or were on) diets. These foods have been forbidden. The bulimics feel powerless to stop during binges. They might feel as though they're in a trance, or hypnotized. They ignore any feelings of fullness or discomfort. They feel they must eat until every morsel of food is gone.

PURGING

Purging happens after bingeing, when bulimics feel guilt and remorse over what they have just done. They must get rid of the food they have consumed. Purging usually takes the form of self-induced vomiting.

February 1, 2007

From the Pages of USA TODAY

Study: Binge eating is No. 1 food disorder in USA; Causes obesity, other problems

Binge eating disorder—frequent, uncontrolled bouts of eating without purging—is the most common eating disorder in the USA, more widespread than anorexia nervosa or bulimia nervosa, according to the first large-scale national survey on these conditions.

The binge disorder, which afflicts 3.5% of women and 2% of men and lasts an average of eight years, can lead to severe obesity, says lead researcher James Hudson, director of the Psychiatric Epidemiology Research Program at McLean Hospital in Belmont, Mass.

Such people eat large amounts of food in short periods of time at least twice weekly. They feel out of control when they are overeating, Hudson says. "Binge eating disorder may explain in part why it's so difficult for some people to control their weight" and why some become severely obese, he says.

A 5-foot-6 [168 cm] woman is severely obese if she weighs 248 pounds [112 kg] or more; a 5-foot-9 [175 cm] man falls in this category if he weighs 270 pounds [122 kg] or more, he says.

Hudson and colleagues analyzed data from about 3,000 people who were asked about their mental health in face-to-face interviews in a separate national study. Findings in the journal *Biological Psychiatry*:

- About 0.9% of women and 0.3% of men said that at some point in their lives they have had anorexia nervosa, which is self-starvation. It lasted an average of 1.7 years.
- 1.5% of women and 0.5% of men said they have had bulimia nervosa, the binge-and-purge disorder that often involves self-induced vomiting. It lasted an average of 8.3 years.
- Fewer than half the people with the disorders got treatment.
- People with the eating disorders often have other mental health problems.

Researchers may ultimately discover that eating disorders, anxiety disorders and mood disorders share a common biological abnormality such as a chemical imbalance in the brain, Hudson says.

—*Nancy Hellmich*

www.usatoday.com

USA TODAY

News

SECTION A

June 9, 2004

From the Pages of USA TODAY

Obesity craze's dangerous message: Size, not health, counts

If roughly 15% of adolescents have been deemed "obese," it's worth bearing in mind that about 5% suffer from anorexia nervosa and bulimia, according to Michael Levine, a psychologist at Kenyon College in Gambier, Ohio. He is a leading specialist in eating-disorders prevention.

Moreover, it is plausible that some overweight kids are merely the flip side of the coin, in which the currency is image and they binge-eat and crash-diet and lose control of their weight. "Obese girls are more likely to report binge-eating or extreme dieting," Levine says.

A study published by Harvard [University] researchers in the journal *Pediatrics* last year found that kids between the ages of 9 and 14 who were dieting without medical supervision gained weight over a three-year period. Kids who weren't concerned about their weight maintained it evenly.

—Patricia Pearson

Bulimics might vomit after any meal or snack, not just after a binge. Bulimics might use a finger or an object to tickle the back of the throat to start the gag reflex. When done on a daily basis or even more frequently, vomiting becomes easier. Many bulimics are able to vomit at will. If it becomes difficult, they might drink something to make them vomit, such as dish soap or another cleaning liquid. These cases usually end up in the hospital.

Bulimics are ashamed of their vomiting and always try to hide it. Some people vomit into bags or napkins and then sneak them out to the garbage. They run the water in the bathroom to try to cover up the sounds they make when vomiting. Some vomit in the shower. If they want to purge in a restaurant, they wait until the restroom is completely empty. Because vomit has a distinctive odor, bulimics use breath mints or gum to hide the smell. Some even carry a toothbrush and toothpaste wherever they go.

MISUSE OF LAXATIVES, WATER PILLS, AND DIURETICS

The digestive system processes the food we eat and turns it into energy. It also gets rid of any waste matter. Food moves from the esophagus to the stomach where it is digested. The digested food moves into the small bowel and then into the large bowel. The large bowel absorbs water as the digested food passes through and stool gradually forms. The stool is stored in the rectum until it is ready to be passed through a bowel movement.

Laxatives stimulate the large bowel. These drugs come in pills, capsules, and liquids. If misused, they can be dangerous. Bulimics who use laxatives believe that they can prevent their bodies from absorbing food by fast elimination. That belief is wrong. Nutrition from food is absorbed in

People who take laxatives frequently develop a tolerance and must take more the next time for the laxative to work.

Warning Signs of Eating Disorders

Because someone with an eating disorder almost always tries to hide it, it is often difficult to notice until there is drastic weight loss. In those with bulimia, it is even harder to detect. Here's what to look for:

- Loss of menstrual period

- Dieting obsessively when not overweight

- Claiming to feel "fat" when overweight is not a reality

- Avoiding a widening range of foods

- Avoiding food until certain hours

- Anger at others if pressed to eat something

- Fear of overeating or gaining weight from a particular meal or type of food

the small bowel, and laxatives work mainly in the large bowel. The small bowel is very efficient at absorbing nutrients, no matter how quickly the food moves through the system. Laxatives do not affect the absorption of calories. The only weight a person "loses" with a laxative is water.

If someone uses laxatives frequently, they will develop a tolerance. This means that they need to take more for the laxative to work. This is why bulimics often overuse laxatives. Overuse can cause inflammation of the intestinal lining, damage to the colon, and severe dehydration. It can also lead to decreased levels of potassium

- Preoccupation with food, calories, nutrition, and cooking
- Not being available for family meals
- Denial of hunger
- Excessive exercising; being overly active
- Frequent weighing
- Secretive or ritualistic eating
- Foods, especially carbohydrates, disappearing quickly from the house
- Fifteen percent or more below normal body weight; rapid weight loss
- Depression
- Slowness of thought; memory difficulties
- Hair loss
- Social withdrawal

and sodium, which are important nutrients. Ironically, overuse of laxatives can also cause constipation.

Bulimics often overuse enemas, a liquid that causes evacuation of the bowel. As with laxatives, enemas can cause rectal irritation and dehydration. Bulimics will take pains to hide their laxative and enema use. They clean the toilet bowl rigorously after defecating and spray air freshener.

Some bulimics take diuretics, which are also known as water pills. These draw excess fluid from the body and turn it into urine. They produce weight loss by removing water, not food or calories.

Diuretics can be dangerous. They lead to dehydration through excessive urination. Most diuretics are prescription drugs, although some herbal formulas are available.

OVEREXERCISING

Excessive exercise can be a symptom of anorexia or bulimia. It is a type of purging behavior. Compulsive exercise means abnormally repeated exercise. It is well beyond what is considered safe or

For anorexics and bulimics, exercising can become a purging behavior over which they have no control.

healthy. Many bulimics will find time and even disrupt other activities to exercise. Like vomiting, they may do it in secret—at night when everyone is sleeping or in a bathroom. The goal is to "undo" the damage from a binge. People with eating disorders often feel tremendously guilty when they eat anything, not just during a binge. They will exercise excessively to punish themselves and burn the calories. This exercise is never enjoyable. Bulimic athletes find no satisfaction in their performance.

On the surface, excessive exercise can seem positive. The person may express a desire to get into shape, eat healthier, and lose a normal amount of weight. But this is never the real objective. Exercise, like starving, bingeing, and purging, gives bulimics a sense of control over their lives. It is another way to relieve stress and guilt. Over-exercising can be addictive. It may become more important than friends, family, school, and just about anything else.

To stay fit, the average person needs twenty to thirty minutes of activity four or five times a week. When people feel they need to exercise, no matter what else they're doing or where they are, they are obsessive.

Joint pain, swelling, and stiffness are common in people who overexercise. Stress fractures of the bones in the feet or shins may develop from too-frequent running or hard walking. When combined with food restriction, osteoporosis is a significant risk. Dehydration, the loss of the menstrual cycle, and heart and reproductive problems can all result from excessive exercise.

CHAPTER THREE

CAUSES OF ANOREXIA AND BULIMIA

Eating disorders are caused by a combination of internal and external forces. The causes may be biological, as in individuals who have a family history of eating disorders. The causes may be emotional, including perfectionism or hypersensitivity. Researchers also blame the media in Western society for providing unrealistic images that young people try to imitate.

BIOLOGICAL FACTORS

Until a few years ago, people assumed biological factors weren't connected to eating disorders. In 2006 scientists confirmed that eating disorders tend to run in families. For example, if your mother or sister had anorexia, you are twelve times more likely to develop it. If only one of them had bulimia, you are four times more likely to develop it. If one identical twin has an eating disorder, her twin has a much greater chance of developing the same disorder.

When scientists studied the brains of people with anorexia and bulimia, they discovered that neurotransmitters (chemicals that help brain cells communicate) played a large role. Researchers in the United Kingdom found that 70 percent of anorexic children and adolescents showed signs of abnormalities with their neurotransmitters. In brain chemistry, certain receptor cells receive certain neurotransmitters. When the two cells attach, a signal goes out. This signal either allows or prevents a message to be passed on to other cells. Signals work together to control functions such as mood, memory, and appetite. In the brains of people with eating disorders, these signals may have an imbalance that causes them to misfire. Doctors hope that these discoveries will lead to the development of drugs to help people with eating disorders.

THE ROLE OF SEROTONIN

Serotonin is a type of neurotransmitter. It affects many behaviors, including hunger, sleep, impulse control, aggression, anger, depression, anxiety, and perception. If someone has low levels of serotonin, he or she might be depressed, aggressive, or even suicidal. High levels of serotonin might lead to high anxiety, insomnia, or an obsession with doing everything perfectly. Changes in serotonin levels can cause serious problems.

Many doctors think that low levels of serotonin can lead to bingeing. Serotonin levels rise during a sugar and carbohydrate binge, so the depression lifts. The opposite is also true. If there is too much serotonin in the brain, a decrease in food would help calm the person.

It is important to remember that biological factors alone do not lead to eating disorders. External factors usually trigger the disordered eating behavior. Many people with low or high serotonin levels do not develop eating disorders.

HORMONES

Hormones are chemicals that control the functions of different tissues and organs. The hormones that control the thyroid and reproductive regions affect things such as stress and appetite. Abnormal levels of these hormones have been found in the brains of people with anorexia and bulimia. Doctors are unsure whether such hormone abnormalities help cause an eating disorder or are the effects of one.

Cortisol, a brain hormone that controls stress and anxiety, is sometimes at abnormally high levels in the brains of people with eating disorders. Leptin, a hormone that controls appetite and weight, is sometimes low. Researchers have found that leptin signals

Life
SECTION D

February 20, 1998

From the Pages of USA TODAY

Two newly discovered hormones in the brain switch on hunger

Drugs made from the hormones ultimately could serve as appetite boosters for people with AIDS or anorexia, while drugs that block the hormones could lead to prescription diet pills, says lead researcher Masashi Yanagisawa of Howard Hughes Medical Institute and the University of Texas Southwestern Medical Center, Dallas.

The hormones were named orexin-A and orexin-B, from the Greek word for "appetite," *orexis*. They appear to be part of a complex system designed over millennia to make sure that people eat enough to sustain them during lean periods.

Yanagisawa says more research will be needed to figure out exactly how this process works. "These hormones," he says, "are a plausible basis for some experiments on eating habits. The question is: What happens in the brain to control highly complex feeding behavior and body weight?"

—*Steve Sternberg*

the brain and other organs when energy levels are dangerously low. Leptin is produced by the body's fat tissue and then released into the bloodstream. In people with very little or no body fat, leptin levels drop. This drop affects a female's menstrual cycle. And this in turn can affect thyroid function and put her at high risk for osteoporosis.

"You can only eat 700 calories a day."

If Emma defied the voice, she was not allowed to eat anything at all the next day. She was obsessed with food. She kept a diary of what she ate and what she would eat in the next week. Sometimes she would dream about the foods she used to love to eat.

Sometimes Emma felt as though her mind and body were at war. She knew she was starving. She felt exhausted all the time. Her clothes were practically falling off her. She began to wear the baggiest clothes she could find. When her friends asked her why she was wearing sweatshirts and sweatpants every day, she began avoiding them.

When her friends called, Emma wouldn't answer the phone. Her mother was in a world of her own, working two jobs. Her father didn't seem to notice anything.

Emma would deliberately walk past bakeries. She would salivate at the sight of layer cakes, cream pies, cookies, and fresh bread.

"Yum-m-m! Don't those look delicious? Well, too bad. You can't have any. You don't deserve them. You don't deserve to eat any food. You're too fat."

Sometimes Emma went into the bakery and bought a cookie. She would take a bite, chew it, and then spit it out.

"If you swallowed any of it, even one crumb, it counts. You have no willpower. You are spineless and weak."

One day she looked in the mirror and could count her ribs. She felt proud of herself.

"What are you so proud of? You're still fat. And fat means failure."

Emma had never failed at anything before.

She would not fail at being skinny.

PSYCHOLOGICAL TRAITS

People who suffer from anorexia or bulimia share certain psychological traits. In some cases, these characteristics exist before the disorder develops. In others, they appear afterward. In either case, these feelings are strong and ever present. They overwhelm the sufferer from the moment she wakes up until the moment she goes to sleep.

NEGATIVITY AND EMOTIONAL SENSITIVITY

Many people with eating disorders have an internal dialogue they call a voice. This voice, which many call Ana or Mia, criticizes them. It tells them how terrible and stupid they are, how everything they do is wrong, and how fat they are. This voice overwhelms every positive thought or move and reinforces an anorexic's lack of self-esteem. It tells her, "You have no value. You are hated. You are ugly." The voice constantly compares her to others and points out her bad traits. It tells her that she is worthless and undeserving of any pleasure. The anorexic does not believe people if they compliment her and feels that people are being nice only because they feel sorry for her.

The voice inside an anorexic's head immediately cancels out any positive remarks. The voice tells her that she is responsible for everyone's unhappiness. It makes her feel as though she cannot control anything and that everything in her life is spinning out of control. The voice then commands her to refuse food. This makes her thinner and punishes her at the same time.

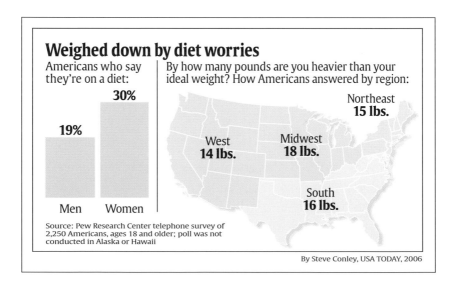

Weighed down by diet worries

Americans who say they're on a diet:

- Men: 19%
- Women: 30%

By how many pounds are you heavier than your ideal weight? How Americans answered by region:

- Northeast **15 lbs.**
- West **14 lbs.**
- Midwest **18 lbs.**
- South **16 lbs.**

Source: Pew Research Center telephone survey of 2,250 Americans, ages 18 and older; poll was not conducted in Alaska or Hawaii

By Steve Conley, USA TODAY, 2006

Anorexics and bulimics are very judgmental toward themselves and others. They may have extreme mood swings and perceive the world as black and white. There is rarely any middle ground. If the anorexic eats something she has decided is forbidden, she will feel as if she is the worst person in the world. When she loses weight, she is the best person in the world.

A person with an eating disorder might take everything personally. She might assume that everyone is judging her. It's hard for an anorexic to be positive. She also might feel that everything around her is somehow her responsibility. If her parents have a fight, it's her fault. She may feel that anything that has ever gone wrong, such as a divorce or an accident, is her fault. She feels guilty and punishes herself. An anorexic wants to control her life and the lives of those around her. When she cannot, she blames herself and takes refuge in the one thing she can control: the food she eats. She believes that everything will change when she loses weight.

A person with an eating disorder may feel that they are the cause of problems between other family members.

PERFECTIONISTS

Perfectionists find fault with everything. This trait is strongly associated with eating disorders. Perfectionists learn early in life that they are valued and measured by their achievements—in school, sports, or even social circles. As a result, the person's self-esteem is completely dependent on other people's approval. She believes that she cannot be loved simply for who she is, flaws and all. She is loved for what she can do and her level of success in the outside world. Perfectionism puts tremendous pressure on a person to excel in all aspects of life.

Perfectionists also think that everyone else can achieve success with little effort. Anorexics often feel inferior. As these feelings increase, they grow out of proportion and distort the anorexic's self-image. Self-esteem is destroyed.

OTHER CONDITIONS RELATED TO ANOREXIA AND BULIMIA

People who suffer from anorexia or bulimia often have other psychological disorders. In some cases, the eating disorder is a symptom of another disorder. In others, the different disorder may be a symptom of the eating disorder. Not everyone with anorexia or bulimia suffers from other disorders. It is important for treatment to address all the underlying issues.

DEPRESSION

Depression is a mood disorder. Symptoms of depression include feelings of worthlessness, sadness, irritability, inappropriate guilt, lack of motivation, and disturbed sleep. Depression can range from the "blahs" to complete despair and hopelessness. Anorexia and bulimia are usually accompanied by depression. If the depression becomes severe enough, a person might have suicidal thoughts.

Depression is both a symptom of and a contributing factor to anorexia and bulimia.

Many people who suffer from anorexia or bulimia have depression in their families.

OBSESSIVE-COMPULSIVE DISORDER

In obsessive-compulsive disorder (OCD), a person is preoccupied by thoughts, feelings, ideas, or actions. Compulsions are the irresistible urges to perform certain acts over and over again. Obsessive thoughts cause the person to worry, and the compulsive behavior reduces the anxiety. Many people experience some level of obsession and compulsion. But these two impulses do not disrupt their lives. When the obsessions and compulsions take over, the person is said to have OCD.

OCD occurs often with anorexia and bulimia. Obsessive thoughts might focus on food, weight, self-doubt, or body image. People with

OCD plus an eating disorder may be obsessed with losing weight. They may have a fear of overeating and a compulsion to exercise, purge, binge, or use laxatives. Some sufferers report that their obsessions take up 90 percent of their time.

"Not under 100 pounds (45 kg) yet. You're still fat."

Emma got off the scale. She was 102 pounds (46 kg). She was determined to be less than 100 pounds (45 kg). She was now exercising compulsively. She had set up a rigid schedule that she would do first thing in the morning and before she went to bed: five hundred jumping jacks, four hundred push-ups, three hundred sit-ups, and forty-five minutes of running in place. She developed scabs on her lower back from doing sit-ups on the rug. She wore several layers of bandages. Eventually she developed calluses.

Her period had stopped a few months earlier. She was glad. It meant she was really skinny. And she loved her cheekbones. They jutted out like a supermodel's. She kept pictures of superskinny models under her pillow and pulled them out to gaze at them.

Her parents were upset about how she looked. So she pretended to eat when they were around. One of her tricks was to make sure her cup was empty at dinner. Then she could hold the food in her mouth, pick up the cup, and spit the food into it. She also dropped food on the floor.

When she ate anything, her stomach began to hurt and bloated up.

"You're fatter than ever. Look at that stomach. You'll never be skinny. What a loser."

Emma would go into her room, close the door, and gaze at the supermodels. They were the only ones who understood.

"You don't deserve to look at those pictures. You're fat. You're fatter than all of them. You're allowed to look at them when you get to 95 pounds (43 kg)."

Emma put her pictures in a drawer.

BIPOLAR DISORDER

People with bipolar disorder suffer from extreme moods. They swing back and forth between depression and mania. Mania is the opposite of depression. A person in a manic state feels unusually happy and positive. Instead of feeling worthless, the person has enhanced self-esteem. When experiencing a manic period, the person might have difficulty sleeping or might talk very fast. Mood swings can lead to impulsive behavior that the sufferer later regrets. Doctors have found that people with anorexia and bulimia are more likely to have bipolar disorder and vice versa.

ATTENTION DEFICIT/HYPERACTIVITY DISORDER (ADHD)

A person with ADHD is generally unable to pay attention and is hyperactive and impulsive. Studies show a possible connection between ADHD and anorexia and bulimia. One similarity between the two conditions is that people who suffer from them are often very impulsive. And like eating disorders, ADHD can produce very negative thoughts, anger, and anxiety.

ADDICTIVE OR SELF-DESTRUCTIVE BEHAVIORS

Anorexia and bulimia are expressions of low self-esteem. They are an unhealthy means of coping with stress and emotional pain. People with eating disorders are sometimes self-destructive—they wish to cause harm to themselves.

Self-destructive behaviors can include cutting, self-mutilation, or self-inflicted violence (SIV). People behave this way because they feel it is easier to cope with physical pain than with emotional pain. SIV is a way of coping with shame, stress, or anger. It can serve as a release for negative emotions that have built up inside. SIV behavior can include cutting, burning, punching, slapping, hitting oneself, biting, head banging, and eating disorders.

THE MEDIA

Many people blame mass media for an increase in eating disorders. The unrealistic notion of beauty seen in movies, on television, and in magazines is never the only reason someone becomes anorexic or bulimic. But the media promotes thinness as the ultimate in physical beauty and that can be a contributing factor along with biological and psychological causes.

www.usatoday.com

USA TODAY

Life

SECTION D

July 18, 1997

From the Pages of USA TODAY

Naomi Wolf blames 'social dysfunction'

Feminist author Naomi Wolf had her own battle with anorexia when she was 12. She wrote passionately about the topic in *The Beauty Myth*. Wolf stopped starving herself, she said when the book was published in 1991, because "I did not want to die. That—and my anger—saved me."

She took her cause and her anger to Capitol Hill last Thursday, to appear at a briefing held by Rep. Louise Slaughter, D-N.Y. The congresswoman is sponsoring a bill to create a national hot line for those who suffer from eating disorders, plus increased educational programs for the public.

"We need," says Wolf, 35, "a national campaign warning girls about the lethal consequences of eating disorders"

that is on a par with programs to fight drug abuse.

In the last five or six years, Wolf says, the public awareness of the problem has "skyrocketed."

Wolf downplays the multiple causes for eating disorders that many experts cite, ranging from a need for perfection to authoritarian parents. She says the public's attention is shifting away from a focus on personal failure or family dysfunction. Those reasons "made a lot of sufferers feel crazy and self-hating," she says.

Instead, Wolf stresses to Congress and her readers that the disorders are caused by "a social dysfunction, unhealthy ideals of thinness portrayed in the mass media."

—*Karen S. Peterson*

EARLY IMAGES

Although the media does not cause eating disorders, it is often the trigger. Because Americans are so influenced by popular culture, they learn at a very young age that fat is bad. They learn that being overweight means you are not pretty, you will not be popular, or you won't get a boyfriend. It means you will be a failure. As a result, the number of cases of eating disorders in girls younger than eight years old is growing.

Media images also cause girls to think of themselves as sexual objects, valued only for how they look. They may not understand why they want to look like the girl in a magazine. They just know they want to. By reading the magazine, they can learn the cover girl's beauty and dieting secrets. But most people do not usually look like people on television and in magazines.

Increasingly, young girls and boys show signs of eating disorders, such as obsessing about looks, weight, and food.

www.usatoday.com

USA TODAY

News

SECTION A

January 8, 2007

Weighty Matters

The causes [of anorexia and bulimia] are complex, but one factor is thought to be the glorification of such super-thin celebrities as Nicole Richie (who reportedly weighed just 85 pounds [39 kg] at a December DUI [driving under the influence of alcohol] arrest) or Ana Carolina Reston, the skeletal Brazilian model who died in November from complications of anorexia.

The Council of Fashion Designers of America is now taking a stand. Its new recommendations to designers include identifying models with eating disorders and providing nutritious snacks. The approach is a far cry from what Madrid [Spain] did last year when it banned too-thin models (those with a body mass index below 18) from the catwalks. And it's nowhere near as drastic as Italy's Chamber of Commerce for Fashion, which wants to require models to keep a healthy weight and get a license from a committee of doctors, nutritionists and other experts.

But even the weaker U.S. approach, taken in response to public pressure, reinforces what hopefully will become a trend. Much like the gradual move against smoking, what's needed is for it to be sustained.

More healthy-looking role models can help. But the answer for the obese and the emaciated is the same: moderation.

USA TODAY Snapshots®

Weight heavier on girls' minds

How important kids say it is to be a healthy weight:

Boys **Girls**

	Boys	Girls
Extremely important	24%	36%
Very important	26%	26%
Important	33%	27%
Somewhat important	12%	9%
Not at all important	4%	2%

Source: Harris Interactive online omnibus survey of 1,487 U.S. youth ages 8-18 Aug. 16-24 on behalf of America on the Move Foundation; sampling error of ±3 percentage points.

By Tracey Wong Briggs and Suzy Parker, USA TODAY, 2006

BODY IMAGE DISSATISFACTION AND SELF-ESTEEM

Although people might tell us that we look fine and that most models and actresses are underweight and unhealthy, it is hard to feel secure about how we look. Very few realistic role models are found in the media. As a result, it can be very hard for people to feel secure and happy with their bodies.

For healthy living, young people need a positive body image. A recent Australian study showed that more than 85 percent of girls between the ages of eleven and eighteen were unhappy with their bodies and were doing something about it. Girls may think that their hips are too large or their breasts are too small. Most people can accept that no one is perfect. People who develop eating disorders, however, cannot. They believe that the physical body is the key to happiness and self-worth. People with eating disorders believe that everything would be better

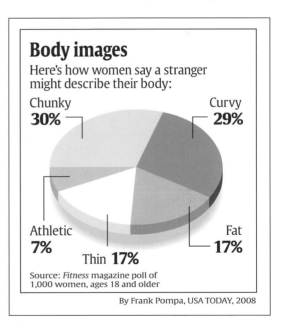

if they looked like a model. These feelings of inadequacy start to filter into every other part of their lives—school, work, and relationships.

PRO-ANA AND PRO-MIA WEBSITES

In the late 1990s, websites were created for anorexics and bulimics to connect with one another. These are called pro-Ana (pro-anorexia)

www.usatoday.com

News
SECTION A

October 24, 2008

From the Pages of USA TODAY

Dangerous 'Model'

Even by reality show standards, MTV reached a new low when it began casting calls for a new show called *Model Maker*. It was seeking women ages 17 to 24 who needed to lose weight. After 12 weeks of intense weight loss, exercise and makeovers, one of the 15 chosen could become a model and win $100,000.

The *Model Maker* concept was in a class apart for its potential to do damage to a vulnerable audience. The reason? It encourages anorexia nervosa, the third most common chronic illness in adolescent females.

Although the causes of self-starvation are complex, the promotion of super-thinness by the fashion world is believed to help trigger and perpetuate it in vulnerable adolescents, the age group MTV targets. The condition, suffered by as many as one in a hundred Americans, has one of the highest death rates of all mental illnesses.

Thankfully, MTV is nixing the show after complaints from, among others, the National Association of Anorexia Nervosa and Associated Eating Disorders and a British parliamentary [law-making] group. The outcry is the latest hopeful marker that society's attitudes to unnatural thinness are slowly changing, much as smoking has become socially dubious.

The shift was on display, too, at last month's New York Fashion Week, where models were sizes 2 and 4, not 0 and less, because the fashion elite is bowing to the growing movement against "heroin chic." In Europe, painfully thin models are banned from some catwalks. And, in May, another reality show chose a plus-size model as its winner.

Some marketers are going one admirable step further and holding up different—and more attainable—beauty ideals. Dove's Campaign for Real Beauty is one of the best-known, with commercials using real women as models, not only the super thin or the young. That's a far healthier message for the MTV generation.

and pro-Mia (pro-bulimia) sites. Some of the sites have become outlets for people who deny that anorexia and bulimia are disorders. These people view the conditions as lifestyle choices.

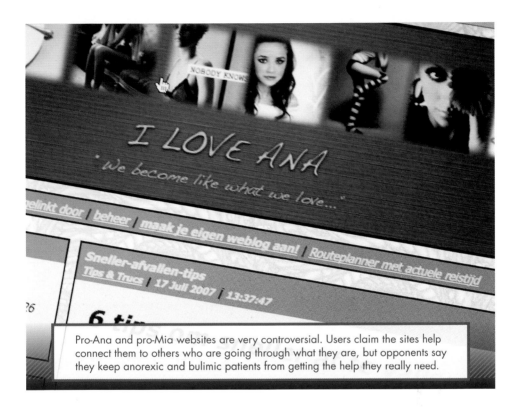

Pro-Ana and pro-Mia websites are very controversial. Users claim the sites help connect them to others who are going through what they are, but opponents say they keep anorexic and bulimic patients from getting the help they really need.

In 2008 doctors in Great Britain called for social networking sites such as Facebook and MySpace to censor their pro–eating disorder pages. They had found that people exposed to the sites felt more negative, had lower self-esteem, perceived themselves as heavier, and were more likely to compare their bodies to others.

Sam sat on the locker-room bench, in shock over what he had done. "I ate out of a garbage can! What is happening to me? What if someone saw me? I am disgusting." He never felt so miserable and depressed in his life.

Even making his weight after he threw up didn't make him feel any better. He felt desperate, confused, and exhausted.

Sam's throat ached after he finally drank some water. He had a terrible taste in his mouth. Coach had brought in some fresh fruit and protein bars. Sam took one bite and felt nauseous. He just wanted to finish his match and go back to his room and sleep.

But Sam's match did not go well. He couldn't seem to get his bearings. He was slow and clumsy. Coach was yelling at him. But Sam could barely hear him. He felt as if he was moving in slow motion, as if someone else was wrestling in his body and he was merely observing. He lost the match. He was ashamed of his wrestling performance and because of what he'd been doing to his body.

That night he called his parents.

The alarm went off at five in the morning Emma tried to open her eyes. All she wanted to do was sleep. But she was cold, even though she was under her comforter and two blankets. Her face was warm, though. Although Emma didn't realize it, she'd started growing a fine layer of hair on her face.

"Get up! You lazy, fat pig! Get up and do your exercise!"

Emma got out of bed, making sure to gather all the hair she was losing on her pillow so her mother wouldn't see it. Her teeth chattered even though she was wearing a sweat suit. She had worn two spots on her floor from running in place. Her mother had forbidden her from exercising in the house. So she jogged in the neighborhood and got back before her mother was even awake. She liked being in the dark. That way, no one would stare at her.

"They're staring because you're so fat."

She got on the scale and smiled: 93 pounds (42 kg). She ran to the dresser and pulled out the drawer with her pictures.

"Put those back. You are not one of them. You're fat. You should have pictures of fat girls. That's what you are."

Emma left the house. She could barely run. She felt so tired. She just wanted to lie down on the side of the road and go to sleep.

"Keep going."

A few people were up at this time of day. Her neighbor, Mr. Greton, waved to her as he picked up his newspaper. Emma looked down. She didn't want him to tell her mother she was out.

She couldn't go very far because she was too weak. The voice was screaming, but she ignored it. She had to go home. She had to go back to bed.

Suddenly Emma felt a slash of pain through her chest. It was excruciating.

"You didn't listen to me! This is what you get!"

Then everything went black.

People with anorexia and bulimia go to extremes to control their weight and attain what they see as their ideal body type. Their role models are often people in the media. Popular culture promotes the unhealthy notion that being extremely thin is beautiful. But most people have to starve themselves to look like models or actors. People with eating disorders who hide what they are doing from their families and friends find comfort online. Pro-Ana and pro-Mia websites provide a place for people to speak openly about their eating disorders. Often, participants cheer each other on, essentially encouraging their virtual friends to stay sick. Health-care professionals are looking for ways to decrease the number of these so-called online "support" groups.

CHAPTER FOUR

WHO GETS ANOREXIA AND BULIMIA?

*S*am felt as if he were walking on air as he made his way back to his locker. The coach just told him that Robbie Gordon, the star wrestler in the 125 class, had broken his ankle in a snowboard accident. The coach said this would be a great opportunity for Sam to really compete. Instead of being number two in the 140 class, he could be number one in 125. The coach said he thought Sam had the potential to be as good as Cody Goodman, who was dominating a weight class that was 15 pounds (7 kg) below his regular weight. Sam was thrilled.

"But Sam," the coach lowered his voice and leaned over the small desk in his office. "You have to want to do this. You need to have the drive and determination."

"I know, sir," said Sam.

"You must be tough," said the coach. "It's all about toughness. Because the body part that's most important in wrestling is. . . . " He sat back and pointed to his head.

"The brain," Sam finished his sentence. The coach always said this.

"That's right," the coach said, standing up. "Think it over, and let me know what you've decided by tomorrow. We don't have a lot of time, and I'll need to alert the other coach if we make a roster change."

Many people in wrestling believe that if you cut weight to reach a lower class you will have an advantage over your opponent. The idea is that while you're cutting weight, you're also pumping more iron and becoming stronger. And it's best to be the strongest and heaviest wrestler in a class.

Sam was already 5 pounds (2 kg) lighter than he'd been six months earlier. He had been working out daily. He would have to work hard to lose the extra 15 pounds (7 kg).

And he had to do it soon. The first meet was in five days.

For a long time, doctors thought that anorexia and bulimia affected only affluent, white, young women. But this is no longer the case. Although anorexia and bulimia do affect young women more than others, there has been a steady increase in cases in other groups including men, athletes, ethnic minorities, very young girls, and older women.

BOYS AND ANOREXIA AND BULIMIA

The first national study of eating disorders was conducted in 2006 by Harvard University researchers. They found that 25 percent of all anorexics and 40 percent of bulimics were boys or men. The scientists were stunned. Earlier estimates had put the number of men with eating disorders at just 10 percent.

The study showed an increase in all forms of weight control by males. These included dieting and diet product use, purging, and vigorous exercise. White males were the least likely to try to control their weight. Latino males were the most likely. In 1990 Dr. Arnold Andersen published a book titled *Males with Eating Disorders*. He said that women who develop eating disorders feel fat before they begin disordered eating behaviors. But typically they are near average weight. Men, on the other hand, are usually medically overweight before they develop a disorder. In addition, men who are binge eaters or compulsive overeaters are undiagnosed more often than women. This is because society is more accepting of an overeating or overweight man than of an overeating or overweight woman.

Men with anorexia or bulimia also suffer from alcohol or drug abuse more often than women with eating disorders. This may be because young men feel they must overindulge in alcohol to prove their masculinity. Most of the underlying psychological factors that lead to anorexia or bulimia, however, are the same for both men and

women. These include the feeling that life is out of their control, low self-esteem, and a strong sense of inadequacy. Men and boys with anorexia and bulimia, just like female sufferers, are attempting to regain control over their lives.

Boys typically begin disordered eating behavior between the ages of twelve and fourteen. But boys as young as eight years old have been diagnosed. The disorder is often triggered by an obsession with fitness and getting in shape. The boy may feel like a failure because the popular boys are all athletes. Or he may feel pressure to make a team or be a better player. Initially, this behavior seems positive. The boy is simply concerned about having a healthy body and cutting out junk food. He starts to eat less and less, while increasing his exercise.

Males who develop eating disorders usually start out with healthy ambitions of getting in shape. But the ambition becomes an obsession and takes over their lives.

Unfortunately, things get out of control fast. Anorexia is addictive behavior, and once the cycle has started, it's very hard to break.

Parents of boys with eating disorders are much less likely to recognize the problem and often deny it. This means a longer time before the boy can start treatment.

DIFFERENCES BETWEEN BOYS AND GIRLS WITH EATING DISORDERS

Eating disorders in boys usually begin for different reasons from those seen in girls. Most boys' eating disorders do not begin with a diet as they do in girls. Nonathletic boys are less likely to have an eating disorder than those who participate in sports. Nonathletic girls run the same risk as athletic girls.

Testosterone is the male hormone responsible for the development of masculine traits during puberty. One of the definite ways to diagnose anorexia in a girl is if her period stops. In boys there is no such clear-cut symptom. But puberty may be delayed or development may slow down.

Boys start puberty later than girls. So they generally begin disordered behavior about two years later than girls. The reason fewer boys develop eating disorders may be that they are older and more emotionally prepared to deal with their changing bodies. Boys also tend to be less critical of their bodies than girls.

Testosterone may also play a role in the origins of eating disorders in males. Studies have indicated that males with anorexia may have persistent or preexisting problems with producing testosterone.

SHAPE VERSUS THINNESS

Boys often have a different objective when they want to change their bodies. They focus more on the shape of their bodies and less on being thin. Young boys watch television shows featuring action heroes with unrealistic body proportions that are impossible to attain. Thin, hard-bodied male models with highly defined, sculpted muscles and "six-pack" abs grace the covers of men's magazines. Those same photos are billboard-sized in retail stores. Popular baseball and basketball players sometimes take performance-enhancing drugs to increase their strength and muscularity.

Studies have shown that many men and boys who watch television commercials with muscular actors become unhappy with their own bodies. U.S. society's culture of muscularity has been linked to eating disorders and abuse of performance-enhancing drugs.

Most male eating disorders are related to athletic performance. Boys typically obsess about their percentage of body fat. They might develop food phobias based on what will and will not give them a competitive edge. Coaches and team members often encourage unhealthy eating and exercise practices. To avoid being labeled a wimp, many insecure boys will go along with whatever they are told. Athletes who must undergo weigh-ins, such as wrestlers and

Boxer Humberto Soto undergoes a weigh-in before a fight in 2010. Male athletes who have to undergo weigh-ins, such as boxers and wrestlers, are more likely to develop eating disorders.

boxers, are the most susceptible to extreme eating behaviors and exercise regimens.

The emotional force behind an eating disorder is usually the same for boys as for girls. But it might appear in a different way. A boy might think he has to reshape his body or lose weight to excel at a sport. He might believe that his success as an athlete is what gives him value. He might be teased at home or school for being out of shape or overweight. Making the conscious choice to limit what he eats gives him a sense of power over his life.

Males are also much more likely than females to develop muscle dysmorphia. This is a body image disorder in which the individual thinks he is small and weak when in fact he is muscular. Bodybuilders who perceive themselves as small and weak are likely to binge, purge, and use performance-enhancing drugs.

Males run a greater initial health risk from anorexia than females because they naturally have less body fat. This means they will begin to lose muscle and tissue much more quickly than girls. Weight loss is often more sudden in boys, due to their higher metabolic rate.

WHICH MALES GET EATING DISORDERS?

Many men with anorexia and bulimia were overweight as children. Others participate in sports that emphasize thinness. These sports include track, figure skating, and gymnastics. Participation in sports that encourage weight lifting, such as boxing or football, can also lead to eating disorders. Wrestlers often try to lose weight quickly before a match so they can compete in a lower weight class. This habit of rapid weight loss can lead to anorexia and bulimia. Boys who suffer from depression or anxiety are more likely than other boys to have eating disorders. In the gay community, appearance is tremendously important. Many gay men are dissatisfied with their bodies. They develop eating disorders at higher rates than heterosexual males.

DIAGNOSIS AND TREATMENT ISSUES

Eating disorders are difficult to diagnose in males. In general, people do not expect boys to have body image issues. Boys who diet or start behaving strangely about food are often overlooked because anorexia and bulimia are considered "girl" disorders. Boys who are struggling with these problems usually feel intense shame and embarrassment. This makes it difficult for them to admit they have a problem, even with obvious symptoms such as extreme weight loss, bingeing, and purging. Also, the current standards that doctors use to diagnose eating disorders were designed for women. For example, one of the main factors that points to anorexia is amenorrhea (absence of menstruation).

Actor Dennis Quaid battled anorexia after shedding weight to play a man dying from tuberculosis in the film *Wyatt Earp* in the mid-1990s.

Attitudes have slowly begun to change since the publication of the 2006 Harvard study on males and eating disorders. Treatment centers have started specific programs designed for boys and men. Males-only recovery groups allow open discussion of emotional issues. As a result of a growing awareness of the problem among males, a few celebrities have admitted to their problems. Actors Dennis Quaid and Billy Bob Thornton have both talked about their battles with anorexia and bulimia. Quaid's struggle began when he had to lose 40 pounds (18 kg) for a film role. He refers to the disorder as manorexia.

SPORTS AND EATING DISORDERS

Studies show that people who compete at high levels of certain performance sports, such as diving, swimming, and figure skating, are at higher risk for abnormal food behaviors. Other activities that fall into this category are wrestling, jockeying, rowing, running, and dancing. Athletes at risk for anorexia and bulimia include those who feel the pressure of "making weight" to compete, as in wrestling. Coaches often encourage unhealthy eating and exercise habits. Sometimes male athletes must abuse their bodies for the short-term goals of the team. Ironically, these practices can undermine health and athletic performance in the long run.

GYMNASTICS

Slender body size and low body weight are essential for gymnasts. Female gymnasts are particularly prone to abnormal eating and dieting. One in ten male gymnasts also suffers from an eating disorder. The standard height and weight for gymnasts has changed dramatically over the years. In 1976 the average female gymnast was 5 feet 3 inches (160 cm) and weighed 105 pounds (48 kg). In 1992 the average female gymnast was 4 feet 9 inches (145 cm) and weighed 88 pounds (40 kg).

Athletes in sports such as figure skating that value slimness are at higher risk for eating disorders.

Christy Henrich

Christy Henrich grew up in Independence, Missouri, and started taking gymnastics classes when she was eight years old. Soon she was practicing seven hours a day, six days a week. Christy was her coach's prize student. At the age of thirteen, she placed fifth all around in the junior division at the U.S. National Championships. In early 1988, she finished tenth in the senior division.

Then, in March 1988, after a meet in Budapest, Hungary, a U.S. judge told Christy that she was too fat. She needed to lose weight to make the Olympic squad. Over the next several months, the 4-foot 10-inch (147 cm) gymnast reached her goal of 90 pounds (41 kg). But Christy failed to make the 1988 Olympic team. She missed qualifying by a fraction of a point.

Her coaches and parents believe that this setback marked the beginning of her eating disorder. Christy bragged to her teammates that she could exist on three apples a day. She would run in a sweat suit in 95°F (35°C) heat. She developed a number of illnesses and injuries and began to isolate herself.

Christy trained before and after school and was away from home from four thirty in the morning until nine thirty in the evening daily. This made it easy to conceal her eating problems from her parents. When she did share a meal with them, she would finish her meal and then go into the bathroom and vomit.

Christy's coach could see what was happening. He met with Christy and her parents to talk about getting help. Although her family found a psychologist and a nutritionist for Christy, she hated talking to them. In the fall of 1990, she stopped going to the doctors. Her physical deterioration continued. Her coach finally told her that she could not train until she got healthy. Christy retired from gymnastics in 1991 when she was nineteen.

In the months and years that followed, Christy was hospitalized a number of times. "My life is a horrifying nightmare," she once said. "It feels like there's a beast inside of me."

In December 1993, Christy seemed to be recovering.

Christy Henrich, pictured here with fiancé Bo Moreno in 1993, was 93 pounds (42 kg) as a competitive gymnast. She weighted only 47 pounds (21 kg) when she died the next year.

Her final relapse caught everyone by surprise—except the doctors. Dr. David McKinsey, who treated her during the last days, said that Christy had passed "the point of no return."

In July 1994, Christy slipped into a coma. Two weeks later, she was dead of multiple organ failure. She was twenty-two years old and weighed 47 pounds (21 kg).

Several famous gymnasts have gone public with their eating disorder struggles. World champion gymnast Cathy Rigby had a twelve-year battle with bulimia and anorexia. She went into cardiac arrest two times as a result of her anorexia. Rigby recalls that although not as much was known about nutrition when she was a competitor, the coaches told the girls what their weight should be. Rigby weighed about 94 pounds (43 kg) at the time of her Olympic win. She was eating one meal a day to drop her weight to 90 pounds (41 kg), which the coaches set as the mandatory weight. Like many other gymnasts, Rigby had no trouble maintaining that weight until her body started to go through puberty.

Cathy Rigby competes at the 1972 Olympic Games in Munich, Germany. Rigby battled bulimia and anorexia throughout her career.

Before puberty, girls and boys have similar amounts of body fat, about 16 to 18 percent. When girls begin puberty, their hips widen and they gain up to 25 percent more body fat. After puberty, most athletic females (especially gymnasts) try to keep body fat at 18 percent, but it is difficult. Body fat lower than 12 percent can affect bone density and disrupt hormone levels.

News

SECTION A

February 6, 2006

From the Pages of USA TODAY

Tennis no match in student's battle with bulimia

Kelli Heaton Eubanks, a tennis player at the University of Tennessee from 1996 to 1998, gave up her scholarship after her sophomore season because of bulimia.

She received counseling and support from the university's health care system but eventually decided she could not play competitive tennis and win her struggle with an eating disorder at the same time.

Eubanks dropped out of school the second semester of her freshman year, sought help at an in-patient treatment center and returned to Tennessee the next fall. But her bulimia continued, and after competing that season, she walked away from tennis.

"My life was more important to me than tennis was," says Eubanks, 28. "If I wanted to be 100% healthy, I couldn't be a part of the sport anymore."

Eubanks dropped out of college, returned to South Carolina and married her hometown sweetheart in November 1998. It took her a year away from the pressures of competitive tennis to bring her bulimia under control, but she has done it.

No more competitive play

She taught tennis for six years until the first of her two children was born, but she has not played competitively since leaving Tennessee. She speaks to high school and college groups about her struggle.

"Talking about it is very helpful for me, and I think I can help other people," Eubanks says. "I won't steer my children away from tennis or other sports, but I will be very cautious.

"It is a sport, not your life, and you have to remember that."

—*Andy Gardiner*

Competing in gymnastics is extremely demanding. Certain psychological traits help gymnasts to succeed. These include perfectionism, compulsiveness, and high personal expectations. These are also key personality traits associated with eating disorders.

"Way to go, Sam!"

It was his second meet at his new weight, and he had pinned his opponent quickly. Sam was feeling really good. His coach had already told him that if he kept this up, the team would go to the state finals. Even Robbie Gordon, who'd had the snowboarding accident, was on his feet cheering for Sam.

Sam had just made it to 125 pounds (57 kg) at that day's weigh-in. The day before, he'd been 130 pounds (59 kg). It was pretty easy for Sam to drop 5 pounds (2 kg) in a day. He had to admit that he liked the way he looked at this lower weight. He had six-pack abs and clearly defined upper-body muscles. Girls smiled at him more.

He and the other wrestlers talked about cutting weight. Cody told Sam that to lose weight for the weigh-in, he had eaten nothing but a tablespoon of peanut butter the day before. He had also climbed sixty flights of stairs in four layers of clothing. When he felt thirsty, he gargled with water and then spit it out. Swallowing the water could add weight.

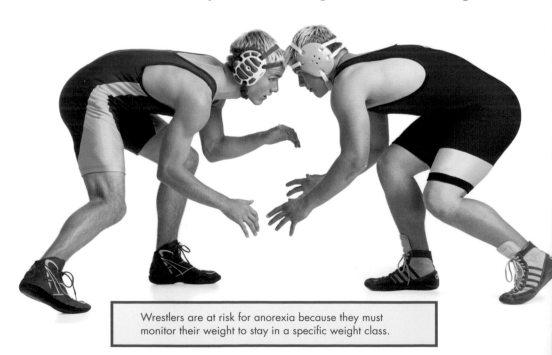

Wrestlers are at risk for anorexia because they must monitor their weight to stay in a specific weight class.

Another wrestler had worn a plastic suit and then jumped rope, sprinted, and kickboxed for over an hour. Someone else had sat in a dry sauna for one-hour intervals and eaten only lettuce for two days. Sam laughed and rolled his eyes with the others. But he did not divulge his secret.

After the meet, the team had their usual pig-out. Everyone was salivating at the thought of it. Someone brought in about twenty pizzas; at least 15 gallons (57 liters) of ice cream; a couple dozen chicken wings; and bags and bags of chips, cookies, and popcorn. They all gorged themselves. This was their reward.

Sam joined in but ate only a little bit at first. It was hard not to stuff himself. But he needed to wait until it was almost time for his mom to pick him up. Then he could be sure he hadn't digested anything. He waited a few more seconds and then lost control, eating everything he could get his hands on.

Soon he'd be home, where he could purge.

WRESTLING

Wrestlers are known for their extreme weight-cutting practices to develop the slim, lean build that the sport demands. Cutting to a lower weight class is thought to give a wrestler an advantage against a smaller opponent. Before weighing in for a match, wrestlers may restrict fluids and calories by fasting, purging, using laxatives, and overexercising. These drastic measures can help wrestlers to lose between 4 and 10 pounds (1.8 to 4.5 kg) within a few days. Wrestlers have reported doing this as often as ten times a season. Participating in this practice can lead to long-term habits and eventually to anorexia and bulimia.

Sam was in his dorm room, trying to write an English lit paper, but he couldn't concentrate. On the bathroom scale, he'd weighed 129 pounds (59 kg), 4 pounds (1.8 kg) over. What was he going to do? The

Athletes and Eating Disorders: What Coaches, Parents, and Teammates Need to Know

The National Eating Disorders Association created some guidelines to increase awareness of warning signs for eating disorders and strategies to help young people avoid developing them.

RISK FACTORS FOR ATHLETES

- Sports that focus on appearance or weight requirements, such as gymnastics, diving, and wrestling
- Sports that focus on the individual rather than a team
- Endurance sports (track and field, swimming)
- Belief that lower body weight will have a positive impact on performance

more nervous he became, the more he needed to gorge himself and then throw up. He was so thirsty. The food wouldn't stay in his stomach, but the water would. He wouldn't allow himself to drink.

Tomorrow Sam would go against the best in the league. He'd won his last four matches, but the one a few days before had been hard. He had tired quickly and knew he wasn't as quick as usual. The guy he was fighting tomorrow was undefeated.

He had taken a laxative the night before, and he would take another one tonight. One of the guys had given him some diuretics.

- Early childhood involvement in a sport
- Low self-esteem, family problems, family history of eating disorders, chronic dieting, traumatic life experiences
- Coaches who focus on success rather than on the athlete as a whole person

HOW TO PROTECT ATHLETES AGAINST EATING DISORDERS

- Use a positive coaching style
- Ensure the support of teammates with healthy body attitudes
- Emphasize using participation in sports as a way to personal success, using motivation and enthusiasm rather than focusing on body weight or shape
- Remember that sports should be fun

So he was urinating like crazy.

The next morning, Sam had terrible diarrhea. It was as if his insides had exploded. His stomach ached. He got on the scale. It showed 127 pounds (58 kg). That was good. He needed to lose 2 pounds (0.9 kg) by that afternoon. Not too bad. He could do it.

He decided to go for a run. He put on multiple layers of clothing and took a new route. He stayed away from the place that made breakfast sandwiches. His head was pounding, and his stomach continued to ache. He was starving. But he couldn't binge, not now.

Suddenly he smelled something wonderful. He stopped and inhaled. It was hamburgers and french fries. He looked around. There was a fast-food place across the street. The smell was so intense. Sam almost felt faint. He ran across the street to be closer. Inside, he could see people sitting at the small plastic tables, eating their food. Sam felt almost a physical stab of envy.

Before he realized what he was doing, he ran around to the back of the restaurant. The dumpsters were off to the side, away from the drive-through window. Sam ran to one of the dumpsters and opened it, grabbing at any food he could find. He shoveled it into his mouth. He didn't even know what he was eating.

EATING DISORDERS AND MINORITIES

Eva walked in the back door after school.

"Hello? Is anyone home?"

She waited a moment. Sometimes her mother loaned the car to her older brother, so even though the car was gone, she was there.

"Mom?"

No reply. Eva unzipped her backpack and took out the plastic grocery bag. She ripped open the bag of chocolate chip cookies and started to stuff them into her mouth, two at a time. She tore open the jumbo Hershey bar and ate it in seconds. She swallowed the candy bar so fast she could barely taste it. She ripped apart the bag of Doritos and began shoveling them into her mouth as fast as she could. She hadn't even taken her jacket off yet.

She heard the car pull into the driveway. Quickly she gathered all the bags of food up and ran upstairs to her room. She shoved the bags under her bed. Many empty bags were under there—empty Doritos bags, cookie bags, a frozen pie carton, an empty ice cream container, and other trash. She'd have to clean it out soon.

News
SECTION A

February 6, 2006

From the Pages of USA TODAY

Athletes' hunger to win fuels eating disorders; Some female college competitors, obsessed with their body image, pay too high a price to stay thin

Kimiko Hirai Soldati, a 2004 Olympic diver, remembers exactly when her bulimia started.

She was transferring from Colorado State to Indiana University, and one day she felt she had eaten too much. "The idea popped into my head that I could get rid of this," she says.

And so she threw up.

That set her on a desperate course. At one point, she says, she was "purging pretty much everything I ate. I was so obsessed about calories that I didn't want to chew gum because there are 5 calories in a stick."

She struggled secretly with bulimia for one and a half years, feeling "shameful and embarrassed" about what she was doing, before she sought out a psychologist who specialized in eating disorders. "When I finally did seek help, I felt like I had a blinking neon sign on my forehead that said 'bulimic, bulimic, bulimic,' and that's all people would see."

—Nanci Hellmich

Kimiko Hirai Soldati enjoys the opening ceremonies at the 2004 Olympics in Athens, Greece. She successfully overcame bulimia.

"Eva?" her mother called from downstairs.

"I'm home," she answered.

"Bean and cheese empanadas for dinner," her mother said. "Your favorite."

"Great," said Eva.

The vomiting was getting easier for Eva. She didn't need to put her finger down her throat anymore. Just bending over brought everything up. She looked at herself in the mirror as she poured some mouthwash into a cup. Her gums were bleeding. Was it from brushing her teeth so often?

For a long time, people believed that anorexia and bulimia affected only young white females. But doctors have learned that it affects all ethnic groups. In fact, evidence shows that Latina and Asian girls feel even more dissatisfied with their bodies than their white counterparts.

Anorexia and bulimia have always been more prevalent in Western cultures, where food is generally plentiful and thinness is more highly valued than in other parts of the world. Besides the United States, eating disorders are common in Canada, Europe, Australia, Japan, New Zealand, and South Africa. In the past, few people reported cases of anorexia and bulimia in areas where food was scarce. Thinness is not as highly valued in countries with a shortage of food. In recent decades, however, Western notions of beauty have been adopted all over the world. Doctors in India and Africa are starting to report cases of anorexia and bulimia.

AFRICAN AMERICANS AND BULIMIA

An important study conducted by the University of Southern California in 2009 presented shocking news. African American girls are 50 percent more likely than white girls to be bulimic. Further, girls from families in the lowest income bracket studied are 153 percent more likely to be bulimic than girls from the highest income bracket.

Before the 2009 study, cases of eating disorders were rare in African American girls. This might be because African American parents are not as sensitive to bulimic behaviors as white parents are or simply because these families have much less access to health insurance. People without insurance do not go for regular checkups and usually don't seek medical advice except in emergencies. Government spending on education is also a factor. Wealthier school

For many years, eating disorder experts thought eating disorders were rare in African Americans. Recent studies have found bulimia is fairly common among African American girls.

districts are able to fund information programs on issues such as eating disorders, while those in low-income communities are not.

YOUNG GIRLS

Adolescence is the most common time for anorexia and bulimia to begin. But the number of cases in all age groups has increased. Cases of eating disorders in prepubescent girls are on the rise. Girls as young as five and six years old may be concerned about weight and body image.

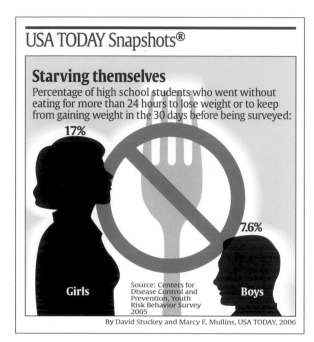

USA TODAY Snapshots®

Starving themselves
Percentage of high school students who went without eating for more than 24 hours to lose weight or to keep from gaining weight in the 30 days before being surveyed:

17%

7.6%

Girls

Boys

Source: Centers for Disease Control and Prevention, Youth Risk Behavior Survey 2005

By David Stuckey and Marcy E. Mullins, USA TODAY, 2006

Gene Beresin, a Harvard psychiatrist, believes that the onset of anorexia has two peaks: one between the ages of ten and thirteen and the other between the ages of thirteen and eighteen. Many girls in the younger group are following examples set by their mothers. The majority of younger children who are overly concerned about their weight have mothers who are worried about their own bodies. Mothers who devote a great deal of time and energy to staying slim can strongly influence their children.

According to recent studies, many girls in fifth and sixth grades have tried to lose weight. This doesn't mean they will all develop anorexia or bulimia. But it does mean that they believe that they can't be attractive unless they are thin. Dieting, purging, and bingeing can cause serious health problems in everyone but especially in young, growing children.

ANOREXIA AND BULIMIA IN OLDER WOMEN

The number of people with anorexia and bulimia who are thirty years old and older has increased in recent years. Some of these people have had eating disorders for many years but have kept them secret.

Or they had eating disorders when they were younger and are suffering a relapse.

The majority of older women recognize that images in the media are unrealistic. But many of them are still not content with how they look. These women may not be able to cope with the normal aging process and the changes in their bodies.

People who make a full recovery from an eating disorder when they are young are not likely to relapse. However, many women will continue to have some degree of lingering signs or symptoms. These can flare up under stress.

Maggie Baumann, who is in her forties, has battled anorexia for much of her adult life.

CHAPTER FIVE

HOW ANOREXIA AND BULIMIA
AFFECT THE BODY

Eva, Jessica, and Sonya were sitting at a small table in the food court at the mall. They had just stopped in the jeans store, and Eva was thrilled that she could fit into a size 1. She knew that Jessica and Sonya were envious.

Eva now alternated between purging and starvation. She was also taking laxatives. She took them only when she was positive no one was at home. It seemed that the recommended dosage worked well only for a while. Lately, she'd had to use three times the dose to get any results.

The vomiting was causing her throat to be sore. That's why she switched to laxatives. Also, her brother was near the bathroom one night when she was throwing up and he heard her. She told him she had the stomach flu. He looked as if he didn't believe her.

"What are you getting, Eva?" Jessica said.

Jessica was looking at Eva's hand. There were old bruises on her knuckles from sticking her finger down her throat. She knew they were talking about her eating habits. She made excuses not to eat lunch with them at school. If she had to, she ran to the fast-food restaurant across the street to vomit. She thought to herself, what's worse: bingeing and purging or eating nothing like those girls she and her friends always made fun of—the skinny ones who ate a saltine cracker for lunch.

"What's wrong with your eye?" asked Sonya.

Eva quickly took out her small purse mirror. She could see something red in the white of her eye.

"I think it's a broken blood vessel," said Sonya. "It happened to my cousin Isabelle."

"Wasn't she the one with bulimia?" asked Jessica.

Sonya nodded. Both girls looked at Eva. Eva needed to change the subject.

"Oh, it's nothing," she said, putting her mirror away. "Want to split some curly fries?" she asked. If I had bulimia, I wouldn't want curly fries, she figured.

Eva couldn't wait until Jessica and Sonya left the mall. They took a different bus home. She waved good-bye and then almost ran to the doughnut shop across the street. She ordered six chocolate doughnuts and devoured them. Then she went into the Chinese restaurant next door. A few minutes later, she was on her knees vomiting in the small, dirty bathroom. As usual, Eva felt great relief. But as she stood up and rinsed her mouth out in the sink, she felt guilt, shame, and fear.

HOW ANOREXIA AFFECTS THE BODY

Anorexia and bulimia lead to malnutrition. A lack of proper nutrition affects every organ and system of the body, especially the brain, heart, kidneys, bones, skin, hair, and intestines.

Dramatic weight loss results in many physical changes. Anorexics usually decrease the amount of carbohydrates, fat, and protein in their diet. They eat very low-calorie foods, such as lettuce and celery, which have almost no nutritional value. Taking vitamins cannot make up for these losses. Over time, this type of diet leads to a decrease of muscle, called muscle wasting. Fluid can build up in the legs. And if there is no protein in the diet, the stomach can swell up. Many anorexics view this swelling as fat and will continue to starve themselves.

BODY FAT

Body weight is divided into three types: bone, muscle, and fat. In a healthy female of average weight, bones make up 12 percent of total body weight, muscle/lean tissue about 35 percent, and body fat about 25 percent. The remaining body weight is skin,

connective tissue, tendons, blood, organs, and so forth. Fat is one of the basic components of the body. It is essential for normal, healthy functioning. Fat keeps us warm by insulating our organs. It is the main source of the body's energy. Fat is part of the structure of cells, which are the basic units of life.

Women have a higher percentage of body fat than men. The extra fat is needed for the breasts, pelvis, hips, and a healthy reproductive system. In men, essential body fat is approximately 10 to 20 percent of the total body weight. In women, it is approximately 20 to 25 percent. Anorexics often have as little as 5 to 7 percent body fat.

Some body fat lies directly under the skin layers. This is called subcutaneous fat. It contains blood vessels, which supply oxygen to the skin. This type of fat also helps to cushion skin against trauma. This fat stores energy, especially during high activity. When subcutaneous fat is lost, the veins in the skin and outline of bones stand out. Weight loss is most obvious in the arms and legs. The body takes on a skeletal appearance. Lack of this kind of fat in the face gives anorexics a gaunt, or sunken, look.

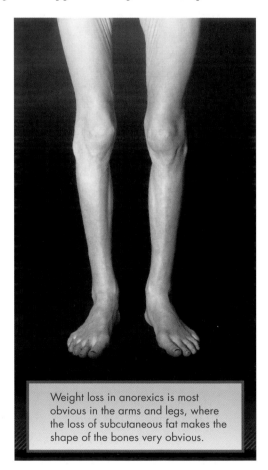

Weight loss in anorexics is most obvious in the arms and legs, where the loss of subcutaneous fat makes the shape of the bones very obvious.

DECREASED METABOLISM AND GLUCOSE

Metabolism converts food and other substances into energy. Metabolic rate is the measure of how efficiently the body works to produce energy. Glucose is the body's fuel. Without it, we cannot survive in good health.

The body obtains glucose through food. Starvation leads to a lack of glucose, which causes a decreased metabolism. This metabolic slowdown causes many body processes (such as the menstrual cycle) to lessen or shut down. Body temperature decreases as the body tries to conserve heat. Anorexics often have temperatures lower than normal and are often cold, even in the summer.

ELECTROLYTES

Electrolytes are essential minerals in the body. They help cells function normally by maintaining an electrical charge across cell membranes. Calcium and potassium are electrolytes. They maintain the electrical currents necessary for a normal heartbeat. The dehydration (lack of body fluid) and starvation that occur with anorexia reduce fluid and mineral levels and cause an electrolyte imbalance.

HEART

Decreased metabolism and an imbalance of electrolytes affect heartbeat and blood pressure. The heart rate of a person with anorexia might drop from a normal 60 to 100 beats per minute to fewer than 60 beats per minute. This lowered blood pressure decreases oxygen to the brain, causing headaches. Anorexics often feel faint or lightheaded, especially when they stand up after lying down for a time. This is because starvation impairs the normal processes of the blood vessels. There might also be a bluish tinge to the hands and feet.

Heart palpitations, or an irregular heartbeat, and chest pains often make anorexics believe they are dying. In severe cases of anorexia,

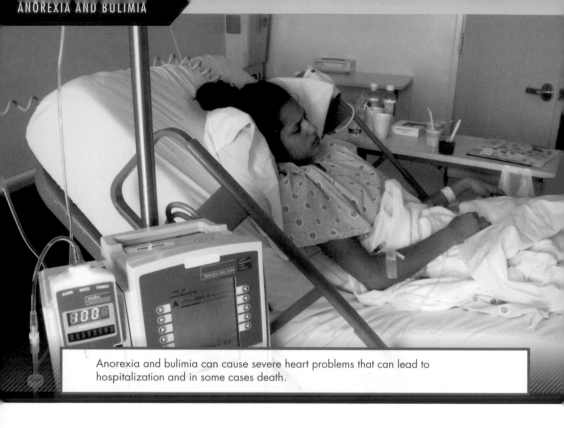

Anorexia and bulimia can cause severe heart problems that can lead to hospitalization and in some cases death.

the heart muscle actually shrinks. Heart disease is the primary cause of death in anorexics.

HORMONES

Hormones are chemicals that bring information to and from cells. Hormones are needed for healthy bones, normal growth, onset of puberty, mood regulation, and energy. Anorexia can delay sexual development by slowing production of the sex hormones: estrogen in females and testosterone in males. If someone with anorexia has not gone through puberty, the condition can permanently alter his or her height. In girls, anorexia may slow or stop breast development and affect their ability to have children.

Thyroid levels are often abnormal, which causes a slower heart rate and constant feeling of cold. Hormones are responsible for amenorrhea, one of the most common effects of dramatic weight loss and self-starvation. Amenorrhea occurs in anorexics because extremely low body weight can interrupt many hormone functions and can stop ovulation (production of eggs). Emotions and mental health also affect hormones, so excessive stress or pressure can cause amenorrhea. Females who are athletes and must train rigorously, such as long-distance runners, gymnasts, or ballet dancers, also often lose their periods due to low body fat, stress, and high-energy expenditure. Often amenorrhea results from several of these factors combined.

OSTEOPOROSIS

Bones are living tissues. The body constantly breaks down old bone and builds up new bone. A healthy diet and exercise make bones stronger. When old bone breaks down faster than new bone is made,

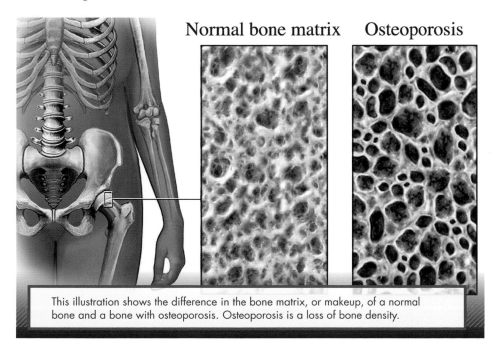

Normal bone matrix   Osteoporosis

This illustration shows the difference in the bone matrix, or makeup, of a normal bone and a bone with osteoporosis. Osteoporosis is a loss of bone density.

bone loss occurs. Poor nutrition and a decrease in body fat can lead to bone loss. Over time, this can cause osteoporosis, a bone disease in which the bones break easily and heal slowly. Osteoporosis is a common and dangerous result of anorexia.

Researchers have found that adolescent anorexics lose more bone density (solidness of bone) than adults with anorexia. When bone density decreases, there is a much higher risk of fracturing or breaking a bone. As we age, our bones weaken, so if individuals lose bone strength in adolescence, they will have problems with weak bones for a long time. Bone fractures in anorexics can result from any high-impact activity, such as running on hard pavement.

SKIN AND HAIR

The anorexic's body adapts to starvation and attempts to maintain its most essential organ functions. But to do this, it withholds nourishment from less essential areas, such as hair and nails. Nails become brittle and skin becomes dry due to lack of protein and fat. Substantial hair loss is also common.

With extreme weight loss, anorexics often develop downy body hair that grows on the back, arms, legs, face, and neck. This is called lanugo. It is the body's attempt at maintaining a normal temperature, since the loss of body fat has robbed it of its natural insulation. This type of hair takes fewer calories to produce than normal hair does.

BRAIN FUNCTION

A lack of glucose can cause the brain to slow down and shrink. Low glucose levels can lead to a lack of memory. Without energy, the brain cannot function properly. Its functions can slow down, leading to seizures and strokes.

At the age of ten, the frontal lobe of the brain is still developing. The frontal lobe rules things such as judgment and organization.

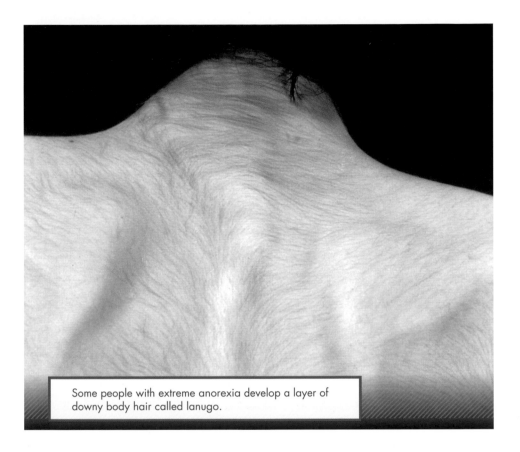

Some people with extreme anorexia develop a layer of downy body hair called lanugo.

Anorexia can delay its development, which can affect the individual's cognitive ability (intelligence). Anorexia's affect on the brain can be permanent.

MENTAL EFFECTS

Anorexics are obsessed with food. They think about it all the time and often prepare high-calorie, high-fat meals for others. Although they have heightened emotional anxiety, they have less physical energy because they eat so little. That combination results in a mental slowdown, distraction, or depression.

Physical Effects of Anorexia

Malnutrition due to anorexia affects every organ and system of the body, especially the brain, heart, kidneys, bones, skin, hair, and intestinal tract. Specific physical affects include the following:

- Loss of menstrual periods

- Lack of energy; weakness, faintness

- Tingling in the fingers and the hands

- Feeling cold all the time

- Dry, yellowish skin

- Constipation and abdominal pain

- Restlessness

- Hair growth all over the body

- Headaches

- Loss or extreme thinning of hair

- Insomnia

EFFECTS SPECIFIC TO BULIMIA

Chemicals in your stomach help to digest food. When stomach contents are brought back up, the chemicals from the stomach irritate the throat. If someone has been repeatedly using a finger to cause vomiting, the nails will scratch the throat and sometimes the roof of the mouth. Repeated vomiting also causes painful cracks in the corners of the mouth, called cheilosis.

Repeated vomiting can also damage the teeth and gums. The acid in the vomit wears down tooth enamel. The gums will become inflamed. Many bulimics brush their teeth immediately after vomiting. This actually wears the enamel down even faster. It also may make gums recede. Dentists can spot a bulimic easily from tooth and gum damage. Some bulimics even require caps on their teeth or oral surgery to repair their gums.

Dr. Gerald Russell, the doctor who was responsible for identifying bulimia, noted scarring on the tops of bulimic's hands. The scars were caused by teeth rubbing on the hands as the person forced the hand back into the throat repeatedly. These scars are called Russell's signs.

Repeated vomiting also causes an enlargement of salivary glands. The parotid glands are in front of and below each ear. When they swell, the person's face looks distorted. Often, even after someone has stopped purging, the glands remain permanently swollen.

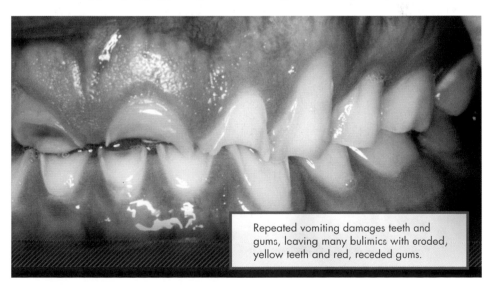

Repeated vomiting damages teeth and gums, leaving many bulimics with eroded, yellow teeth and red, receded gums.

www.usatoday.com

USA TODAY

Life

SECTION D

February 15, 2000

From the Pages of USA TODAY

Magali Amadei says she's lucky to have bad teeth

Seven years of bingeing and purging took a toll on 26-year-old model Magali Amadei. Stomach acids eroded her teeth, resulting in 11 caps, seven root canals and two bridges.

But all that was a small price to pay, the recovered bulimic says. Things could have been worse. She could have damaged her intestines or reproductive organs. She could have died.

"It's amazing to think of all the time and energy I wasted on this. It controlled every second of my life."

Amadei says her bulimia began at age 14, before she was a fashion model. But being in the business made the bulimia a full-time obsession. At her worst, she was bingeing and purging seven times a day and swallowing 40 laxative pills.

"I would wake every morning and think about when I would eat and throw up. I was constantly thinking about food and about how fat I was."

Amadei, who is 5-foot-9 [175 cm], is reluctant to talk about how much she weighed when she finally decided to seek help, because "then others will start to compare themselves to those numbers."

Even now, she refuses to own a scale. "I just can't risk weighing myself anymore. It's too hard."

—*Maribel Villalva*

DAMAGE TO THE STOMACH AND ESOPHAGUS

The esophagus is often affected by repeated vomiting. The muscle that prevents stomach contents from flowing backward into the esophagus is called the lower esophageal sphincter. When the sphincter is weakened, it causes a burning sensation in the chest called heartburn, or reflux. Some people develop sores, or ulcers, in the esophagus. This narrows the esophagus, making it harder to swallow food.

Repeated vomiting can also cause small tears in the esophagus. It can even cause it to burst. If this happens, stomach contents can surround the heart and lungs. Forceful vomiting over a long period of time can also tear the stomach. This causes the contents to flow to the abdominal cavity. Tears in the esophagus and stomach can lead to death.

Smaller tears or irritation in the stomach or esophagus can lead to weakness and fainting. They can also lead to anemia—an abnormally low level of red blood cells. These tears, because they are unseen, can cause internal bleeding. This can be serious and fatal. Stools will turn black if there is internal bleeding.

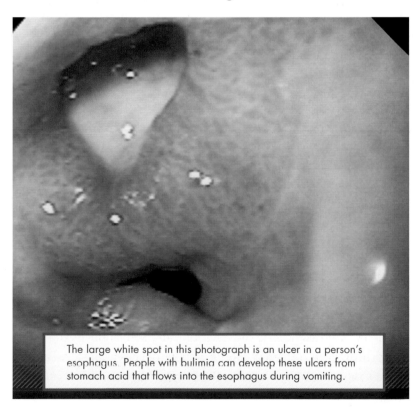

The large white spot in this photograph is an ulcer in a person's esophagus. People with bulimia can develop these ulcers from stomach acid that flows into the esophagus during vomiting.

www.usatoday.com

USA TODAY
Life
SECTION D

June 22, 2006

From the Pages of USA TODAY

McPhee's bulimia was once 'out of control'

American Idol runner-up Katharine McPhee waged a five-year battle with bulimia that she managed to get under control.

"Food was how I dealt with emotions," says McPhee, 22, who says that at one point she would vomit up to seven times a day. "As soon as I would feel something, I would eat."

When she auditioned for *Idol* in August, her bulimia was "out of control." She credits her parents and actor boyfriend, Nick Cokas, 41, for helping when she began a three-month program at L.A.'s Eating Disorder Center of California in October. She reported to the *Idol* set in December. McPhee chose not to tell fellow contestants and had "somebody I would try to go see on a weekly basis" (a therapist) to avoid a relapse.

Although she says she is still healing, McPhee, *Teen People*'s August cover girl, tells the magazine: "I'm really starting to embrace my curves."

—*William Keck*

Katharine McPhee attends an event for *American Idol* in 2006. After *Idol* finished taping, she talked about her struggles with bulimia.

ORGAN DAMAGE

The dehydration and electrolyte disturbances caused by frequent vomiting can damage the heart and kidneys. The risk to these organs is increased with the use of laxatives or diuretics. Electrolytes control the electrical impulses that enable the heart to beat. In a normal heart, these impulses occur at regular intervals. But when electrolytes are out of balance, the heart does not beat regularly. This can lead to an irregular heart rhythm, or arrhythmia. It can also lead to sudden death.

CHAPTER SIX

TREATMENT

Eva was lying on her bed in her room. She was absolutely exhausted. She couldn't get up the energy to start her homework. Her grades at school had gone down. She didn't care. Suddenly she had a terrible pain in her stomach. She pulled her knees up and took a deep breath. Her stomach had been hurting recently. This time was the worst.

She wanted to stop bingeing and purging and using laxatives, but she didn't know how. Her entire life had become controlled by food—eating it, throwing it up, and worrying about it. "I'm a size 0 now," she thought. "But it isn't making me happy."

Eva hated everyone who seemed happy: the blonde, skinny girls; the stupid boys who liked them; and even Jessica and Sonya. Why were they happy? Why was she so miserable? Since she'd started bingeing and purging, she had almost no social life. She worried about what she would eat and where she could throw up. And what if someone she knew walked in on her. She just wanted to stay home—alone.

She went into the bathroom and looked at herself. Her eyes had broken blood vessels. Her cheeks were swollen from inflamed neck glands. Maybe if I throw up, my stomach will stop hurting, she thought. Her mother was downstairs. Eva wondered if her mother knew what she was doing. She gave her a look after Eva had purged. She probably did know.

Eva kneeled on the bathroom floor and retched into the toilet. She grabbed her stomach. The pain was intense. When she looked into the toilet bowl she gasped. There was blood in it.

The door to the bathroom opened.

"Eva!" said her mother. "What's wrong with you?"

The biggest challenge in treating an eating disorder is for the sufferer to recognize that the eating behavior is a problem. People with eating disorders believe that their behavior is a solution to other problems. Most people with anorexia or bulimia deny that they have an eating disorder. As a result, they often do not enter treatment until a physical or mental crisis occurs.

Because eating disorders are a complicated mix of physical and psychological problems, both the mind and body must be treated. The physical effects of an eating disorder cause many of the psychological changes. Food restriction and extreme eating distorts attitudes and emotions. Recovery is a team effort. It involves medical doctors, psychologists, nutritionists, physiotherapists, and exercise therapists.

Getting back to a healthy diet is the first goal. Then work can begin on the psychological disorder.

TREATMENT APPROACHES

If an eating disorder is caught and treated early, there is a good chance of a fast and complete recovery. Unfortunately, this is not what usually happens. Anorexia and bulimia can go undiagnosed for a long time. The sufferers hide their behavior and deny there is a problem. Often the family is in crisis and distracted by other issues.

Once a diagnosis is made, the patient and caregivers choose a treatment approach. No one treatment plan works for all cases. People should investigate all available methods and customize the treatment for the patient. Physical symptoms must be dealt with and proper nutrition restored. Then therapy can begin, either with a group, individually, or with the family.

Where the treatment takes place depends on the severity of the disorder. Some patients can be treated while still living at home. Others must be hospitalized.

When an eating disorder is diagnosed early, patients can remain at home. They attend sessions at a therapist's office for several hours each week. Some patients live at home but attend sessions at a clinic for most of the day. They eat most meals at the clinic. When physical symptoms are more serious, patients may need to be treated at the hospital for several hours each day. In the most serious cases, patients are treated at a facility that specializes in eating disorders. They live in the hospital full-time until it is safe to go home. Patients might stay at these facilities for long periods, from a few weeks to several months.

A person with an eating disorder cannot make important decisions alone. The family must be involved in all treatment decisions. It is also important to find a doctor who specializes in eating disorders. A family doctor or pediatrician without training in eating disorders may not be aware of all the available treatment options. In the best scenario, a team of doctors help to treat people with anorexia and bulimia. The team is led by the eating disorder specialist. A therapist provides

Therapy is an important part of recovery for people with eating disorders.

October 8, 1997

From the Pages of USA TODAY

Notre Dame runner battles eating disorder

JoAnna Deeter believes she has conquered the toughest opponent she will meet. For the Notre Dame cross-country runner, the foe isn't oxygen debt, fatigue or another athlete.

For about four years the sophomore has battled an eating disorder, anorexia nervosa.

Deeter and her parents diagnosed her anorexia before the critical stage. Two years ago as a senior at Eden Prairie (Minn.) High, she checked into a hospital for two months. She was 5' 7" [170 cm] and weighed slightly more than 100 pounds [45 kg]. At November's NCAA championships, she took third overall and was the top freshman in a spectacular and surprising finish.

In battling the problem, Deeter relies on what she calls "my team," consisting of her parents plus a campus group, including her coach Tim Connelly, a sports psychologist, a nutritionist and a doctor. The Notre Dame contingent meets a couple of times a year, with Deeter seeing her coach daily and the psychologist weekly.

Deeter also has founded an eating-disorder group at school to help and to educate victims on campus and in South Bend, Ind.

"I'm vocal, and it's hard for me to see people suffering," says Deeter, who's often approached by victims, especially runners. "I want something positive to come out of this."

Most of all, Deeter feels better, though she realizes the battle might never be over.

—*Dick Patrick*

counseling for patients and their families. A nutritionist monitors the family's meal planning and overall nutrition. Some nutritionists specialize in treating anorexic and bulimic patients.

Eva and her mother were sitting in the doctor's office, waiting.

Earlier, Eva and her mother had seen Dr. Gomez in an examination room. She had told them that Eva had a bleeding stomach ulcer, which was causing the pain and the bleeding. Dr. Gomez said this often happens with bulimia. Eva's teeth were starting to wear down from the acid in the vomit. Her esophagus was very tender. Dr. Gomez said that if Eva's mother hadn't discovered her, Eva could have ended up in the hospital with a ruptured stomach or esophagus. Dr. Gomez said these conditions can lead to death.

Eva felt embarrassed and ashamed. After her mother found her in the bathroom, Eva told her everything. She told her about the bingeing, the purging, and the fasting. Eva's mother had found all the empty bags and wrappers under her bed a few days earlier.

Dr. Gomez walked into the office. Behind her were two other women.

"Eva, Mrs. Garcia, I'd like you to meet Dr. Lampert and Diane Garber. Dr. Lampert is a psychiatrist, and Mrs. Garber is a nutritionist."

Eva's mother looked very upset.

"Eva does not need a psychiatrist," she said.

Dr. Gomez smiled. "Yes, she does, Mrs. Garcia. I suspect Eva is depressed. Her eating disorder is a sign that she is unhappy." Eva said nothing.

"But, I don't understand," said Mrs. Gomez to Eva. "Is this something to do with our family? Are you ashamed of us?"

"No, Eva is not ashamed of you," said Dr. Lampert. "Depression can be caused by many things, and there is often a biological component. Eva needs someone to help her understand why she felt the need to binge and purge. We will help her."

Eva felt embarrassed and ashamed. But she also felt relieved. She'd been keeping her terrible secret for almost two years. She reached over and took her mother's hand.

"Mama, I want to get better. This has nothing to do with you."

Eva's mother smiled.

MEDICAL TREATMENT

There is no single medication that can cure an eating disorder. If medication is used, it is part of a treatment plan that combines therapy and nutritional counseling. Doctors know that malnutrition affects mood and behavior. This can make it difficult to determine if a patient has any underlying emotional issues. It can be hard to tell whether extreme mood changes, sleeplessness, obsessive-compulsive behavior, and other emotional issues point to an underlying personality disorder or if the eating disorder has caused these symptoms. Malnutrition also changes how medicines affect the mind and body.

Antidepressants, which help increase the level of serotonin in the brain, are sometimes prescribed for anorexia and bulimia. It has not been proven that antidepressants help in the initial stages of treating anorexia. But they do seem to help prevent a relapse. Antidepressants have been proven to help in the treatment of bulimia.

Emma awoke in the hospital. Her mother was in a chair next to her bed, sleeping. What had happened? The last thing she remembered was running outside, feeling so tired.

Then she realized there were tubes in her arms. Food! They were feeding her! She yanked the tubes, crying out at the pain.

Her mother woke up.

"Emma! What are you doing? Nurse! Help!"

A nurse ran into the room and tried to hold Emma down. Emma struggled. They could not feed her. They could not. Before Emma knew what was happening, the nurse had given her a shot. Emma felt instantly calm. Her mother came over to her and took her hand.

"Emma? Honey? Do you know you almost died today? You had a heart attack." She began to cry.

Emma had passed out in front of Mr. Greton's house. He called 9-1-1 and Emma's mother. The paramedics had had to revive her. Emma's organs were shutting down.

They arrived at the hospital, and the attendants cut away Emma's sweat suit. Her mother almost fainted at the sight of Emma's arms and legs. She could see every protruding bone in Emma's body. She looked like a picture of a malnourished child from Africa. Her mother was horrified.

How did this happen?

HOSPITALIZATION AND REFEEDING

It may take a life-threatening incident for many people with eating disorders to receive the help they need. Anorexics may experience chest pains, fainting, suffer a heart attack, or attempt suicide. For bulimics, a tear in the esophagus, the stomach, or vomiting blood can be fatal. Hospitalization provides the patient with protection and treatment.

Once an anorexic or bulimic has been admitted to a hospital, doctors will begin returning the patient to normal eating behaviors. This is called refeeding. The toll an eating disorder takes on the body is considerable—lost nutrients; internal damage from purging; and muscle, tissue, and

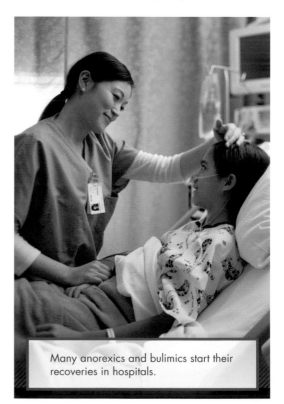

Many anorexics and bulimics start their recoveries in hospitals.

organ reduction. This damage must be repaired before the psychological recovery can begin. Repairing internal damage takes time and patience.

Refeeding can be traumatic for the patient. She does not want to eat. She may be very angry that she is in the hospital and may insist that nothing is wrong. Eating attempts make her anxious and fearful. Refeeding must be done slowly and carefully. The body has adapted to the abnormal eating patterns and is in a fragile state. A rapid change in consumption can worsen electrolyte and other biochemical balances. The shock of food that has been avoided for a long time can cause abdominal pain and bloating.

A nutritionist works with the sufferer to plan a menu that is often a combination of liquid food supplements and solid foods. The nutritionist will try to accommodate the person with "safe foods," or foods that the person enjoys or feels comfortable eating. Doctors recommend a slow refeeding process for an average weight gain of about 2 to 3 pounds (0.9 to 1.4 kg) a week. Someone with anorexia has generally been eating very little—perhaps as few as 500 calories a day. The thought of eating a normal diet, which might contain 2,000 calories a day, is terrifying. So refeeding has to begin gradually and build up.

THERAPY

Therapy is a critical part of treatment. Patients will spend many hours talking to their therapists. One of the goals of therapy is to identify and resolve the issues that triggered the eating disorder. Since many people with anorexia and bulimia have low self-esteem, it is important to learn the reasons why. Therapy provides a safe environment for talking about any topic without fear of consequences. Therapy can also help to identify other disorders that may have led

to the anorexia or bulimia. Depression, OCD, and anxiety often go hand in hand with eating disorders. A therapist can help sort out what problems were caused by the disease and what existed prior to the eating disorder. Each individual situation must be evaluated to determine which type of therapy might be most effective.

PSYCHOANALYSIS

During psychoanalysis, a psychiatrist examines a patient's subconscious mind to discover the roots of a psychological problem. The therapist might interpret dreams and analyze hidden feelings. The goal is to find out why the patient is self-destructive. This type of therapy focuses on problems from childhood or adolescence that might have caused the eating disorder

Cognitive behavioral therapy (CBT) is one of the most widely used therapies in treating eating disorders. A branch of psychotherapy, it is based on the idea that thoughts (cognition) and actions (behaviors) are related. When we change our thoughts, we change our behaviors. Once the relationships between thoughts, emotions, and actions are understood, the patient can replace negative thoughts and emotions with positive ones. The patient can begin to return to a healthy lifestyle. Often therapists will ask individuals to keep a journal or food diary as part of CBT.

CBT teaches patients that family and school are not responsible for their thoughts or behavior. CBT teaches individuals that they are responsible for their own recovery. This kind of therapy can be comforting to individuals who feel that their lives are out of their control.

CBT is designed to be used short term, over six to twelve months. CBT is a well-established and effective treatment for anorexia and bulimia. It also helps with other issues that often accompany these disorders, such as depression, OCD, and anxiety. CBT also teaches individuals how to avoid and tolerate stressful situations and how to deal with stress to avoid a relapse into disordered eating.

THE MAUDSLEY FAMILY-BASED APPROACH

This approach is named for the London hospital where it was developed in the 1980s. It is based on the idea that food is medicine and parents are the best ones to dispense it. Parents are usually the most committed and supportive people in the patient's life.

The Maudsley method is for children or teenagers living at home. It takes the view that the eating disorder controls the patient, rather than the other way around. A patient did not choose to stop eating and is not able to change her behavior. How or why the eating disorder began is not important. This idea is to eliminate blame. Parents must take control from the eating disorder so that it becomes powerless. They alone must make all decisions about their child's eating behavior.

Parental involvement is an important part of the Maudsley method.

The Maudsley method requires a deep commitment from all family members. The child must be monitored full-time for the first few weeks. For parents, this often requires taking time off work. Parents must understand that all responsibility lies with them.

April 6, 2010

From the Pages of USA TODAY

Treatment for binge eating need not be extensive or expensive

A new study offers hope for binge eaters—people who frequently eat an unusually large amount of food in a short amount of time and feel their eating is out of control.

"Some people are very distressed by their bingeing cycles and don't realize it's a treatable condition," says Lynn DeBar, one of the study's authors and a psychologist for Kaiser Permanente.

Researchers recruited 123 people, most of them women, average age 37, and all covered by a Kaiser Permanente health plan. They had at least one binge-eating episode a week. Half of the participants were given some basic healthy eating guidance information and alerted to the relevant health plan services.

The other half attended eight therapy sessions in which counselors taught them strategies outlined in *Overcoming Binge Eating*, a book that offers a six-step self-help program. Findings in April's *Journal of Consulting and Clinical Psychology*:

- After three months, 63.5% of those who received the therapy and the book had stopped bingeing, compared with 28% of the other group.
- At the end of a year, 64% of book-and-therapy patients had stopped bingeing vs. 45% of the others.

"Many binge eaters have given up hope that they could control their eating," says the study's lead author, Ruth Striegel-Moore, a professor of psychology at Wesleyan University in Middletown, Conn. "They often think they have to go through extensive and expensive treatment, but for many, this plan is a simple, cost-effective first step."

—*Nanci Hellmich*

OTHER TREATMENTS

Patients often undergo other types of treatment along with those already mentioned. Other treatment includes physical or occupational therapy, art therapy, yoga, and meditation. Twelve-step programs, life coaches, and biofeedback are other alternatives.

A twelve-step program is a set of ideas that present a course of action for recovery from addiction or behavior problems. The founders of Alcoholics Anonymous were the creators of the twelve-step program. It is used by other people who struggle with addiction. For people suffering from anorexia and bulimia, the steps help them to identify the problem, accept that they need help, and work to find an emotional and behavioral process to begin a new life without obsessing about food.

Meditation is sometimes part of a treatment plan for people with eating disorders.

Life coaching is a motivational program. It inspires people to seek positive changes in their lives. Life coaches are trained to help patients achieve personal and emotional goals.

Biofeedback is a technique that uses special instruments to measure a person's heart rate, brain activity, muscle tension, and skin temperature. It provides information on how a person's body reacts to physical or psychological stress. The idea is that once people are aware of how they feel when they are stressed, they can work to physically change their thoughts and behavior.

The hospital had run a number of tests on Emma. They discovered abnormal heart activity and dehydration. Her heart rate was much slower than normal. During the first few days of hospitalization, she

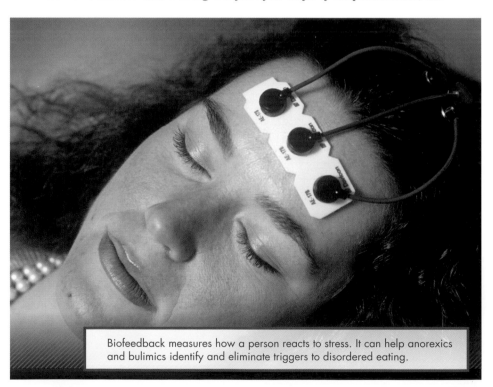

Biofeedback measures how a person reacts to stress. It can help anorexics and bulimics identify and eliminate triggers to disordered eating.

had needed a feeding tube. Then she was trying to eat on her own—a protein shake, a tiny bowl of plain pasta, and some soup. But it was difficult for her. Her throat felt as if it was closing. It took her forty-five minutes to eat a small bowl of noodles. Her stomach hurt and looked horribly bloated. She tried not to look at it or to think it looked fat.

On Emma's birthday, her mother baked her favorite cake: devil's food with butter cream frosting. She cut a small piece. It took her half an hour to finally finish it.

Emma was horribly depressed. She was working with a team of people: a doctor, a psychologist, and a nutritionist. She took several types of medications, including antidepressants. She started to feel better.

The voice seemed to be gone. But Emma worried it would return. Her therapist reassured her that because she was in control of herself and she controlled the voice, it would not return. Emma's parents also met with her therapist, because it was important that they learn to spot danger signs.

Once she went home, Emma did relapse once. With help from professionals, she continues to recover.

CHAPTER SEVEN

RECOVERY

Recovering from an eating disorder is difficult and takes time and patience. It involves more than an end to the bingeing, purging, and food restriction. It means stopping the negative voices, self-hatred, fear, and guilt. Trying to eliminate longtime behaviors and beliefs takes courage, perseverance, and the support of family and friends. There is no "normal" recovery time from anorexia or bulimia.

For people with anorexia or bulimia, their abnormal behavior surrounding food and eating has become normal. In many cases, people suffer from these illnesses for years, often without their friends and families knowing. Through the eyes of someone suffering from anorexia or bulimia, the bingeing or purging or extreme weight loss is positive. Some specialists consider eating disorders to be addictions. Although food is not dangerous in the way that drugs or alcohol are dangerous, the behavior surrounding food for someone with an eating disorder is similar to other addictions. The brain chemistry changes as a result of malnutrition. The person ignores damage to the body from the eating disorder. The eating disorder gradually becomes the most important thing in life. Friends, school, and family all become secondary. Recovery time is quicker for some people than others. It is common to want to return to the unhealthy behavior. For many people, recovering from an eating disorder is a long and difficult struggle.

RELAPSE

Most people with anorexia or bulimia have at least one relapse. It is important to realize that recovery from these disorders is often not an immediate reversal of past behaviors. After anorexia or bulimia is recognized, acknowledged, and diagnosed, a cycle of recovery and relapse may begin. The number of times a person falls back into unhealthy eating patterns and negative thoughts is not important. The patient must not become discouraged. He or she works to identify and eliminate the triggers for abnormal eating behaviors. A good therapist will work to assure patients that recovery is a gradual process with ups and downs. Relapsing does not mean failure.

Symptoms of relapse include weight loss, disordered eating behaviors, and distorted attitudes regarding body weight and shape. Anorexic patients sometimes develop bulimic symptoms during relapse. For people who are being treated for bulimia, it is important to pay attention to overexercising. If someone is in recovery, they have stopped other types of purging and might take up exercise as a healthy way to take care of their bodies. However, this can become a replacement for restriction or purging.

The best way to minimize or prevent relapse is to identify risky situations in advance. Risky situations are usually something external. They can range from a big event—a breakup, for example—to something like the tone of someone's voice. Many people suffering from anorexia or bulimia are extremely sensitive. They often read more into a situation than is intended or overinterpret an innocent remark. If the person in recovery knows that a particular person or situation has caused stress in the past, she can take steps to avoid or better manage the person or situation.

Some people, depending on the type, length, and physical symptoms of their eating disorder, may experience long-term health problems. These can include issues related to infertility, bone density, weakened heart muscle, damage to the digestive tract (usually caused by the misuse of laxatives), and other organ damage.

After Sam's poor performance at the wrestling match, he talked to the coach. He admitted that he'd been purging to cut weight. The coach said he suspected as much. He was sorry that Sam had been compelled to take such extreme measures. Two days later, the coach had two doctors from the campus health service come in for a talk on healthy weight cutting for wrestlers.

Sam started working with a therapist and a nutritionist. Three months later, he is wrestling better than ever. He is in a higher weight class, and it's where he belongs.

Sam also goes to a support group for males with eating disorders. When the doctor explained that he had bulimia, Sam was embarrassed. But the doctor told him that people who participate in certain sports, such as wrestling and gymnastics, have a high risk of developing eating disorders. In fact, when he went to the support group, Sam spotted a gymnast he recognized from the gym. Sam introduced himself, and the two became good friends.

With the help of a doctor and a therapist, Sam has regained his health.

MENTAL HEALTH ISSUES

Some people who have been treated for and recovered from an eating disorder still experience depression, anxiety, or compulsive behavior. The reason is that these mental health issues have always been underneath the anorexia or bulimia. Stopping the disordered eating does not mean the underlying issue is gone. Many times these issues are the reason the eating disorder developed in the first place. Shifting the focus to food restriction or bingeing and purging helped the person avoid these issues. Once the disordered eating behavior is dealt with, the underlying issues can be dealt with openly in a healthy way. Anyone going through recovery work with a therapist will work to understand and manage these other mental health issues.

www.usatoday.com

USA TODAY

Life

SECTION D

July 18, 1997

From the Pages of USA TODAY

Teens tell USA TODAY that they are well aware of eating disorders

About 400 applicants for USA TODAY's Teen Panel wrote the paper about the concerns of young people. About one-fifth mentioned eating disorders. (Panel members will be announced in August.)

"The most pressing concerns of teen-age girls are diet and weight," says Rachel Lynne Levine, 14, El Paso [Texas]. "I believe this is because of the unrealistically thin bodies shown on television and in magazines." Girls are targeted, she says. "Seldom do pictures show the perfect guy who just lost 5 pounds [2 kg] in five days."

Sometimes it feels "as if we have to look like Barbie dolls to get friends, boyfriends, jobs and just plain attention," says Laura Kinkeldey, 15, Tabernacle, N.J.

Kirsten Keeler, 15, Indianapolis [Indiana], says, "Look through the magazines. You can't find anybody who weighs over 120 pounds [54 kg]. It's like it doesn't matter how smart you are, what is on the inside."

Kirsten speculates sometimes the malady is a desperate ploy to get attention. "You want your family to notice you." She and her friends are definitely aware of peers in danger. "But it is not like they will admit to it themselves or know what to do. And we don't have the guts to tell them and try to stop their behavior."

Some teens, says Cody Sohn, 18, Carmel, Ind., actually see an eating disorder as a "status symbol. It is a fashionable thing for some girls to say they have," even if they don't.

Perhaps many of the teen panel applicants have friends who do not actually have full-fledged eating disorders. Instead, they are kids fixated on "body image, losing weight." The obsession is still dangerous, she says. Combined with other risk factors, fixations can easily turn into full-blown eating disorders.

Jenifer Scheyer, 14, Northbrook, Ill., sees an up side to all the corridor talk about anorexia. Her friends like to tell stories about girls and celebrities who "have gotten through it OK. They realize they can be healthy again, and not do that to themselves."

—Karen S. Peterson

For people with anorexia or bulimia, *recovery* is a word that might mean different things to different people. In some cases, recovery means the end of symptoms of an eating disorder (starving, bingeing, excessive exercising, and purging). In other cases, recovery is the end of the physical symptoms and an end to the self-hatred, fear, guilt, and negative voices. Recovery time also differs from person to person.

The goal of eating disorder treatment is full recovery: living life free of eating disorder thoughts and behaviors. Many people think that one is never completely recovered from an eating disorder. This is not entirely correct. Recovery takes time and patience, but it is possible, and many people have achieved it.

The goal for people in treatment is full recovery and a return to everyday life free of the taunts and distractions of Ana and Mia.

EVA

It has been six months since Eva started working with Dr. Lampert and Mrs. Garber. She's taking an antidepressant and is in a support group with other people who have bulimia. At first she was embarrassed, but when she heard other girls talk about their bingeing and purging, she felt less alone. Eva is gaining self-esteem. She realizes that she felt inadequate because she looked different. She is gaining a sense of her self-worth. Her grades are going up again in school, and she feels happier.

Her mother and father were going to a support group for parents of children with eating disorders. The whole family was learning that eating and food are just a small part of bulimia.

Eva is working with Mrs. Garber to eat a healthy diet. It's been difficult, and she has binged and purged a few times. But she knows that relapse is very common and, even more important, not to feel bad and blame herself for it. Eva also knows that she will be prone to bulimia and other eating disorders for the rest of her life. She is learning to recognize the warning signs—depression, shame, and hopelessness— and speak to someone about it to get help.

EMMA

Emma and her parents arrived at the treatment center. It was a beautiful place with a lot of privacy. She didn't know what to expect, but everyone seemed friendly. Emma was assigned to a room on the second floor. It was nicely decorated, with a wide window seat. Emma wondered when she had last read a book. It had been a long time ago.

She was unpacking her suitcase when her roommate came in.

"Hi. You must be Emma. I'm Jane." The small Asian American girl put out her hand. "Welcome."

www.usatoday.com

USA TODAY

Life

SECTION D

July 27, 2004

From the Pages of USA TODAY

Day-to-day things now for Olsen

Actress Mary-Kate Olsen, one-half of Hollywood power siblings the Olsen twins, was discharged from a treatment facility Friday, her publicist said.

Olsen, 18, spent six weeks at the exclusive Cirque Lodge in Sundance, Utah, battling an eating disorder.

"She is feeling very well," spokesman Michael Pagnotta says. "This is still very much an ongoing process."

Olsen's father, Dave, told *Us Weekly* that Mary-Kate has had an eating disorder for two years.

"The average time to be cured, from onset to recovery, is four to seven years," says Doug Bunnell, president of the National Eating Disorders Association. "The family struggle with (an eating disorder) doesn't stop when they leave the hospital."

Pagnotta declined to detail Olsen's treatment plan but says: "She's going to enjoy the rest of the summer doing day-to-day things like shopping, going to dinner with friends and family, and going to movies. She won't be hiding."

Mary-Kate and her twin sister, Ashley, also are reading scripts and preparing for their freshman year at New York University.

—*Cesar G. Soriano*

Mary-Kate *(right)* and her sister, Ashley, appear at a movie premiere in 2004. Mary-Kate underwent treatment for an eating disorder a few months later.

Emma smiled. She felt a little awkward. Jane looked perfectly healthy, with glowing skin and hair. She was slim but not bony. Emma was still under 100 pounds (45 kg). Jane noticed Emma looking at her body.

"When I came here, I weighed 74 pounds (34 kg)," she said. "I've been here for a while. I was on a feeding tube in the hospital for a month. It's been a journey, believe me."

Emma relaxed a little and sat down on her bed.

"Everyone here has been through what you've been through," said Jane. "Restriction, overexercise, and the voice."

"You heard the voice?" Emma asked. It was hard for her to believe it.

Jane nodded. "We all heard it. But not anymore."

Emma started to cry. Jane came over and gave her a hug. "You're on the road to recovery," she said.

GLOSSARY

anorexia nervosa: a life-threatening eating disorder that is characterized by self-starvation and excessive weight loss

attention deficit hyperactivity disorder: a disorder characterized by inattention, hyperactivity, and impulsivity

bingeing: consuming an unnaturally large quantity of food in a short period of time; eating uncontrollably

biofeedback: a technique in which people are trained to improve their health by learning to control certain internal bodily processes that normally occur involuntarily, such as heart rate, blood pressure, muscle tension, and skin temperature

bipolar disorder: a disorder wherein people suffer from extreme moods, swinging from depression to mania and back again

bulimia: repeated overeating binges followed by compensatory behavior, such as forced vomiting or excessive exercise

cortisol: a brain hormone that regulates stress and anxiety

dehydration: the loss of water and salts from the body

depression: a mood disorder that is usually expressed by feelings of worthlessness, sadness, irritability, inappropriate guilt, lack of motivation, and disturbed sleep

diuretics: medication that works to remove fluid from the body through urination

eating disorder: extreme emotions, attitudes, and behavior surrounding eating, food, and weight issues

electrolytes: minerals in the body that conduct electricity and are found in the body, fluid, tissue, and blood

emaciation: a wasted condition of the body; extreme thinness

esophagus: a hollow, muscular tube that starts in the throat and ends at the stomach

fasting: abstaining from food

genetics: the study of heredity, the process in which parents pass certain genes onto their children

glucose: a type of sugar found in the blood that is used for energy

hormones: chemicals released by cells that affect cells in other parts in the body

hysteria: a medical term that is used to refer to a state of extreme fear or emotion and irrational behavior

lanugo: a fine, downy body hair on backs, arms, legs, the face, and the neck

leptin: a hormone that regulates appetite and weight

malnutrition: when the body does not get enough nutrients

mania: the opposite of depression; a state of extreme happiness and energy

metabolism: all the physical and chemical processes in the body that create and use energy

neurotransmitter: a chemical in the brain used as a messenger from one nerve cell to another

obsessive-compulsive disorder: a disorder wherein obsessions (recurrent and intrusive thoughts, feelings, ideas, or actions) constantly occupy the mind of the sufferer

osteoporosis: a disease in which the density and quality of bone are reduced

pro-ana/pro-mia: nicknames for the promotion of anorexia (ana) or bulimia (mia)

purging: self-induced vomiting or defecating

refeeding: restarting nutrition to someone with an eating disorder

relapse: when someone who is getting treatment for a problem slips back into the disordered behavior or thinking again

restriction starvation: limiting food to an extreme degree

serotonin: a hormone in the brain that communicates between nerve cells; a neurotransmitter

testosterone: a male hormone that regulates many physiological processes in men

twelve-step program: a set of guiding principles outlining a course of action for recovery from addiction, compulsion, or other behavioral problems

RESOURCES

Eating Disorder Recovery
http://eatingdisorderrecovery.com/

This informative website is dedicated to helping those with eating disorders to navigate their personal eating disorder recovery.

Eating Disorders Publications and Education
http://www.bulimia.com/

This website provides expert information and resources about eating disorders, bulimia, anorexia nervosa, and binge eating disorder.

ED Recovery
http://edrecovery.com/

This blog is for women who are struggling with anorexia, bulimia, and compulsive eating.

National Eating Disorder Information Center
200 Elizabeth Street
Toronto, ONT M5G 2C4
866-NEDIC-20
http://www.nedic.ca/index.shtml

This Canadian site provides help, support, and information on eating disorders.

National Eating Disorders Association
603 Stewart St., Suite 803
Seattle, WA 98101
800-931-2237
http://www.nationaleatingdisorders.org/

The National Eating Disorders Association provides information and resources on eating disorders, including a kit for parents and families, links to treatment centers, referrals to health professionals where you live, and much more.

Something Fishy: Website on Eating Disorders
866-690-7239
http://www.something-fishy.org

This exhaustive site is dedicated to providing awareness and support to people with eating disorders.

SELECTED BIBLIOGRAPHY

ABC News. "Young Girls Start Eating Disorders Early." Preventdisease.com. N.d. http://preventdisease.com/news/articles/disorders_start_early.shtml (July 15, 2009).

Armenian Medical Network. "Eating Disorder May Be Missed in Boys, Non-Whites." Health.am. May 14, 2007. http://www.health.am/psy/more/eating-disorder-may-be-missed-in-boys/ (August 12, 2009).

Bennett, Jessica. "It's Not Just White Girls." *Newsweek*, September 6, 2008. http://www.newsweek.com/id/157574 (July 15, 2009).

Blinder, Barton J., and Karin H. Chao. "Eating Disorders: A Historical Perspective." In *Understanding Eating Disorders*, edited by LeeAnn Alexander-Mott and D. Barry Lumsden, 3–36. Washington, DC: Taylor and Frances, 1994.

Boskind-White, Marlene, and William C. White Jr. *Bulimia/Anorexia: The Binge-Purge Cycle and Self-Starvation*. 5th ed. New York: W. W. Norton & Co., 2001.

Brumberg, Joan Jacobs. *Fasting Girls: The History of Anorexia Nervosa*. New York: Vintage Books, 2000.

Bulimia Help. "I Feel Like Bulimia Is Part of Who I Am." BulimiaHelp.org. March 3, 2009. http://www.bulimiahelp.org/community/forums/i-feel-bulimia-part-who-i-am (August 3, 2009).

Carlton, Pamela, and Deborah Ashin. *Take Charge of Your Child's Eating Disorder: A Physician's Step-by-Step Guide to Defeating Anorexia and Bulimia*. New York: Da Capo Press, 2006.

Collin, Laura. *Eating with Your Anorexic: How My Child Recovered through Family-Based Treatment and Yours Can Too*. New York: McGraw-Hill, 2004.

Elliott, Victoria Stagg. "Look beyond Stereotypes to Spot Patients with Eating Disorders." *American Medical News*, April 20, 2009. http://www.ama-assn.org/amednews/2009/04/20/hll20420.htm (July 30, 2009).

GoodTherapy.org. "Ana: A Story about Making an Ally with One's Anorexia." GoodTherapy.org. November 1, 2007. http://www.goodtherapy.org/blog/new-story-added-to-the-healing-story collection-ana/ (August 12, 2009).

Gordon, Richard A. *Eating Disorders: Anatomy of a Social Epidemic*. 2nd ed. Malden, MA: Blackwell Publishers, 2000.

Heartsupport. "Guys Have Eating Disorders Too." Heartsupport.com. August 26, 2008. http://www.heartsupport.com/blogs/eatingdisordersstories/guyshaveeatingdisorderstoo.html (August 1, 2009).

Heaton, Jeanne A., and Claudia J. Strauss. *Talking to Eating Disorders: Simple Ways*

to Support Someone with Anorexia, Bulimia, Binge Eating, or Body Image Issues. New York: New American Library, 2005.

Hepworth, Julie. *The Social Construction of Anorexia Nervosa*. Thousand Oaks, CA: Sage Publications, 1999.

Heywood, Leslie. *Dedicated to Hunger: The Anorexic Aesthetic in Modern Culture*. Berkeley: University of California Press, 1996.

Katzman, Debra K., and Leora Pinhas. *Help for Eating Disorders: A Parent's Guide to Symptoms, Causes and Treatment*. Toronto: Robert Rose, 2005.

National Eating Disorders Association. "Health Consequences of Eating Disorders." NationalEatingDisorders.org. N.d. http://www.nationaleatingdisorders.org/p.asp?WebPage_ID=286&Profile_ID=41143 (August 22, 2009).

Nicholas, Sadie. "Confessions of a Middle-Aged Anorexic." *Mail* (London) Online. April 24, 2008. http://www.dailymail.co.uk/femail/article-1016645/Confessions-middle-aged-anorexic-How-eating-disorders-affecting-older-women-too.html (July 17, 2009).

Pascoe, C. J. "'You're Just Another Fatty': Creating a Pro-Ana Subculture Online." Digital Youth Research. January 22, 2008. http://digitalyouth.ischool.berkeley.edu/node/104 (July 21, 2009).

Random History. "A Fear of Food: A History of Eating Disorders." RandomHistory.com. August 8, 2008. http://www.randomhistory.com/2008/08/08_eating.html (July 22, 2009).

Real Mental Health. "The Genetics of Anorexia and Bulimia." RealMentalHealth.com. August 2005. http://www.realmentalhealth.com/eating_disorders/genetics.asp (August 3, 2009).

Science Daily. "Adolescent Girls with ADHD Are at Increased Risk for Eating Disorders, Study Shows." March 15, 2008. http://www.sciencedaily.com/releases/2008/03/080314085032.htm (July 13, 2009).

Sherman, Roberta. "How to Know When a Young Athlete's Exercise Is a Problem." *Eating Disorders Today* 5, no. 4 (2007). Available online at http://www.bulimia.com/client/client_pages/nl_edt_5_4_1.cfm (July 20, 2009).

Stacey, Michelle. *The Fasting Girl: A True Victorian Medical Mystery*. New York: Penguin Putnam, 2002.

Stanford, Peter. "Sister Marie Thérèse: 'Anorexia Has Been a Friend.'" Independent.com. January 27, 2008. http://www.independent.co.uk/news/uk/this-britain/sister-marie-thregravese-anorexia-has-been-a-friend-773791.html (August 10, 2009).

Student Nutrition and Body Image Action Committee. "Eating Disorders." SNAC. N.d. http://www.snac.ucla.edu/pages/Body_Image/Eating_Disorders.htm (August 13, 2009).

FURTHER READING AND WEBSITES

Anderson, Laurie Halse. *Wintergirls*. New York: Viking Juvenile, 2009. This emotion-packed novel traces the descent of Lia through her battle with anorexia.

Costin, Carolyn. *The Eating Disorders Sourcebook: A Comprehensive Guide to the Causes, Treatment, and Prevention of Eating Disorders*. New York: McGraw-Hill, 2006.

Hautzig, Deborah. *Second Star to the Right*. New York: Puffin, 1999. Hautzig's own battle with anorexia gives this gripping novel about the self-destructive behavior of an anorexic named Leslie the ring to truth.

Hyman, Bruce M., and Cherry Pedrick. *Anxiety Disorders*. Minneapolis: Twenty-First Century Books, 2006.

———. *Obsessive-Compulsive Disorder*. Minneapolis: Twenty-First Century Books, 2009.

Langley, Jenny. *Boys Get Anorexia Too: Coping with Male Eating Disorders in the Family*. London: Paul Chapman Publishing, 2006.

Littman, Sarah. *Purge*. New York: Scholastic Press, 2009. Janie, who suffers from bulimia, goes through rehab after her eating disorder comes to light.

Menzie, Morgan. *Diary of an Anorexic Girl*. Nashville: Thomas Nelson, 2003. Menzie uses diary entries to profile her hard but ultimately successful battle against anorexia.

Nelson, Tammy. *What's Eating You? A Workbook for Teens with Anorexia, Bulimia and Other Eating Disorders*. Oakland: New Harbinger Publications, 2008.

Orr, Tamara B. *When the Mirror Lies: Anorexia, Bulimia, and Other Eating Disorders*. New York: Children's Press, 2007.

Paterson, Anna. *Running on Empty: A Novel about Eating Disorders for Teenage Girls*. Bristol, UK: Lucky Duck Publishing, 2002. Three friends develop different eating disorders as a means to cope with problems they are facing. Ultimately, they work together to help one another get well again.

INDEX

ABOUT THE AUTHOR

Carol Sonenklar's first young adult books were inspired by her two children. She has since written about a wide range of subjects including health, the environment, and popular history. She enjoys translating complex topics into understandable and engaging writing. Carol is also an editor and specializes in helping writers for whom English is a second language. Carol loves to hike with her two dogs in the mountains. She currently lives in Colorado.

PHOTO ACKNOWLEDGMENTS

The images in this book are used with the permission of: © Steve Hamblin/Alamy, pp. 1, 3; John Heller AP/USA TODAY, p. 8; © FPG/Hulton Archive/Getty Images, p. 15; Lynne Mcafee/Rex USA, p. 19; Everett Collection/Rex USA, p. 21 (left); Rex/Rex USA, p. 21 (right); © Kitaeva Tatiana/Shutterstock Images, p. 28; David Levenson/Rex Features USA, p. 33; © David J. Green-Lifestyle/Alamy, p. 37; © Barsik/Dreamstime.com, p. 40; © Profimedia International s.r.o./Alamy, p. 47; © Penny Tweedie/Stone/Getty Images, p. 49; © Tom Grill/Corbis; Premium RF/Alamy, p. 53; ANP PHOTO BY KOEN SUYK/Newscom, p. 57; © Simon Winnal/Taxi/Getty Images, p. 62; © Jed Jacobsohn/Getty Images Sport/Getty Images, p. 64; © Robert Hanashiro/USA TODAY, p. 66; © Ryan McVay/Allsport Concepts/Getty Images, p. 67; AP Photo/Kansas City Star, Kelley Chin, p. 69; © Bettmann/CORBIS, p. 70; © Photodisc/Getty Images, p. 72; © Robert Scheer/USA TODAY, p. 77; © Custom Medical Stock Photo / Alamy, p. 79; Mark Avery/Orange County Register/Newscom, p. 81; © Biophoto Associates/Photo Researchers, Inc., p. 84; © Hola Images/Alamy, p. 86; Phototake/Newscom, p. 87 (bottom); Custom Medical Stock Photo /Newscom, p. 89; © 2010 Edward H. Gill/Custom Medical Stock Photo, p. 91; © David M. Martin, M.D./Photo Researchers, Inc., p. 93; © Dan MacMedan/USA TODAY, p. 94; © Oliver Voisin/Photo Researchers, Inc., p. 98; © rubberball/Getty Images, p. 102; © Design Pics. Inc/Alamy, p. 105; © Angela Hampton Picture Library /Alamy, p. 107; © Will & Deni McIntyre/Photo Researchers, Inc., p. 108; © Monkeybusiness/ Dreamstime. com, p. 114; © Peter Kramer/Getty Images/USA TODAY, p. 116.

Front cover: © Steve Hamblin/Alamy.